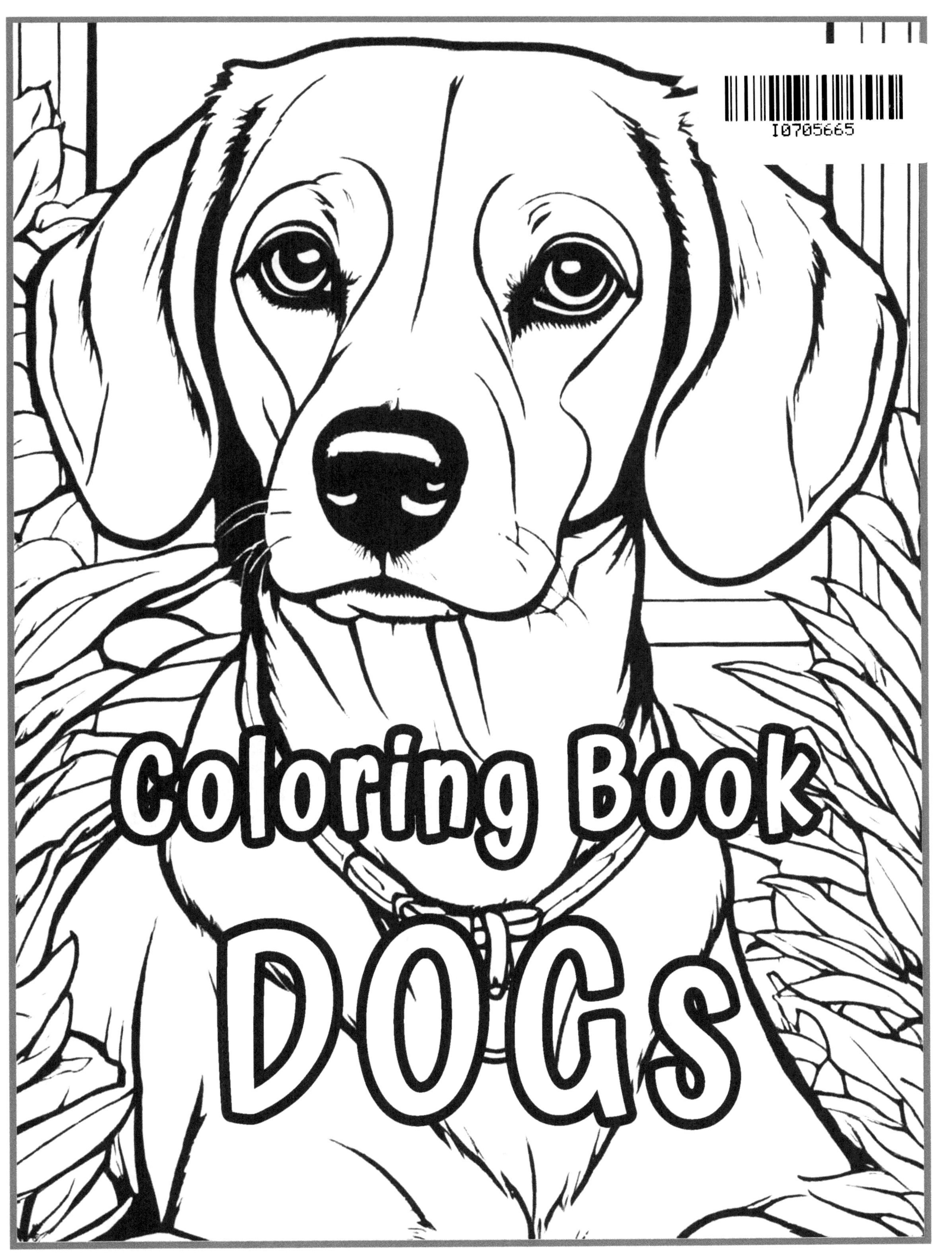
Coloring Book
DOGS

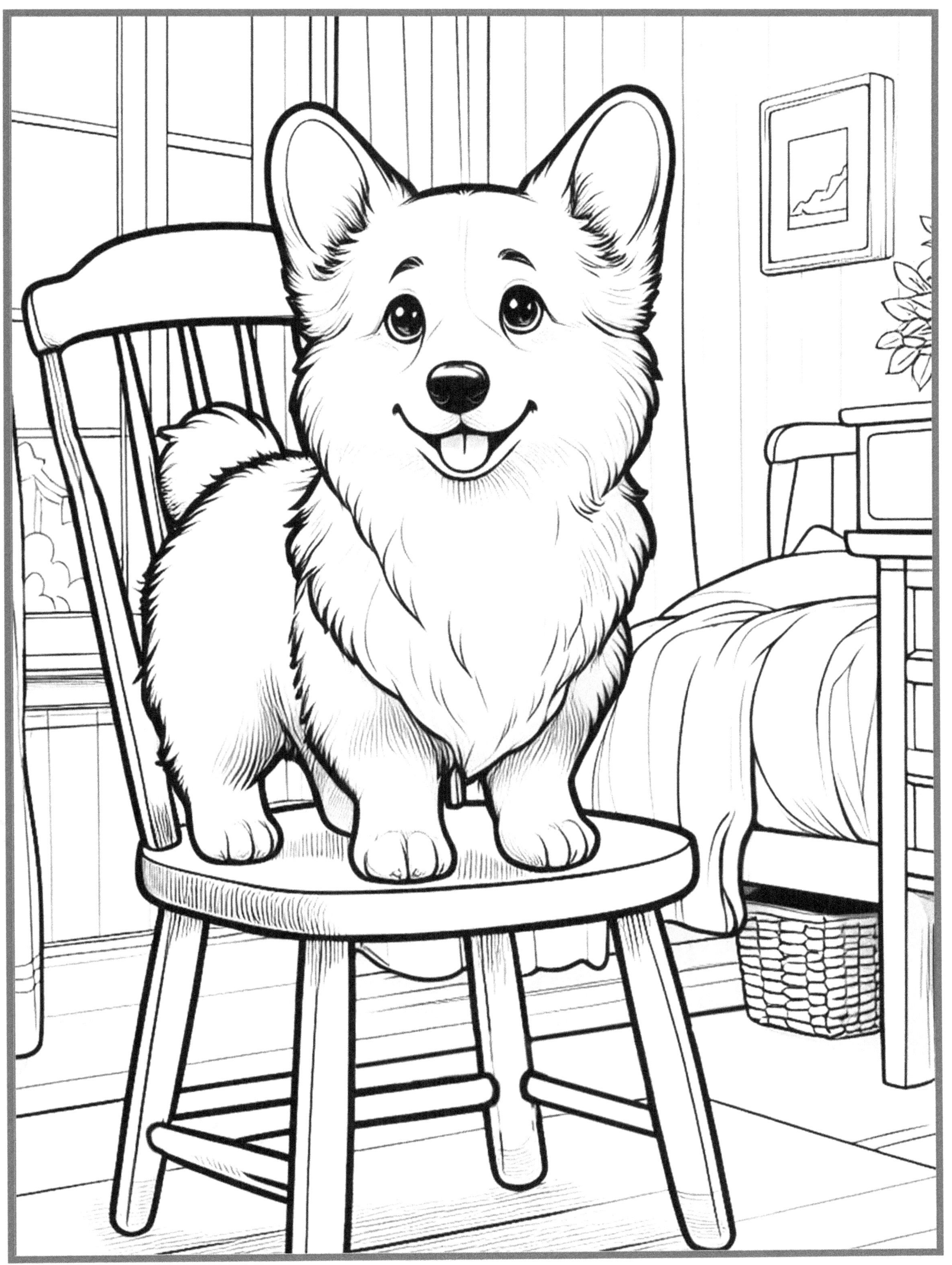

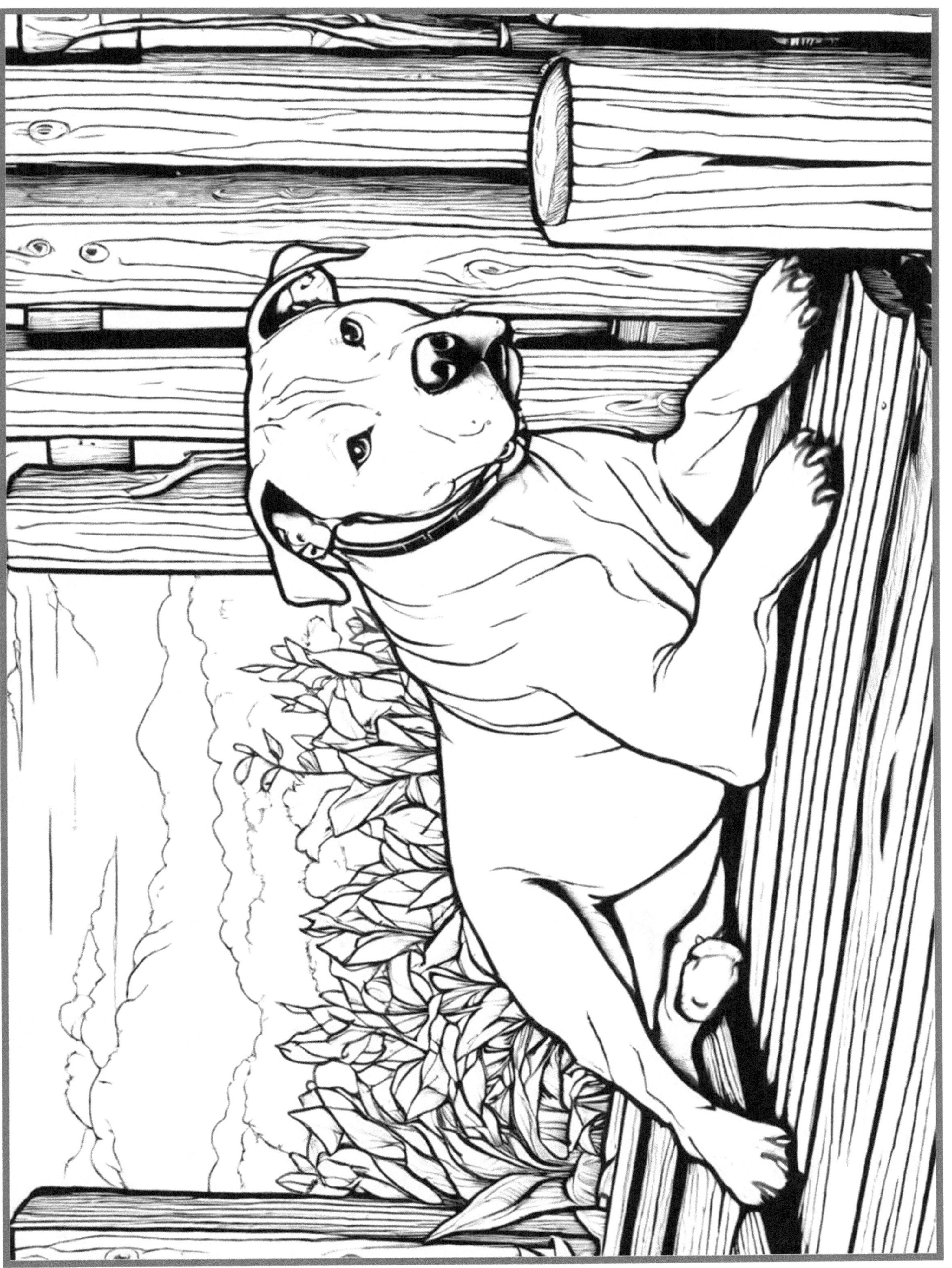

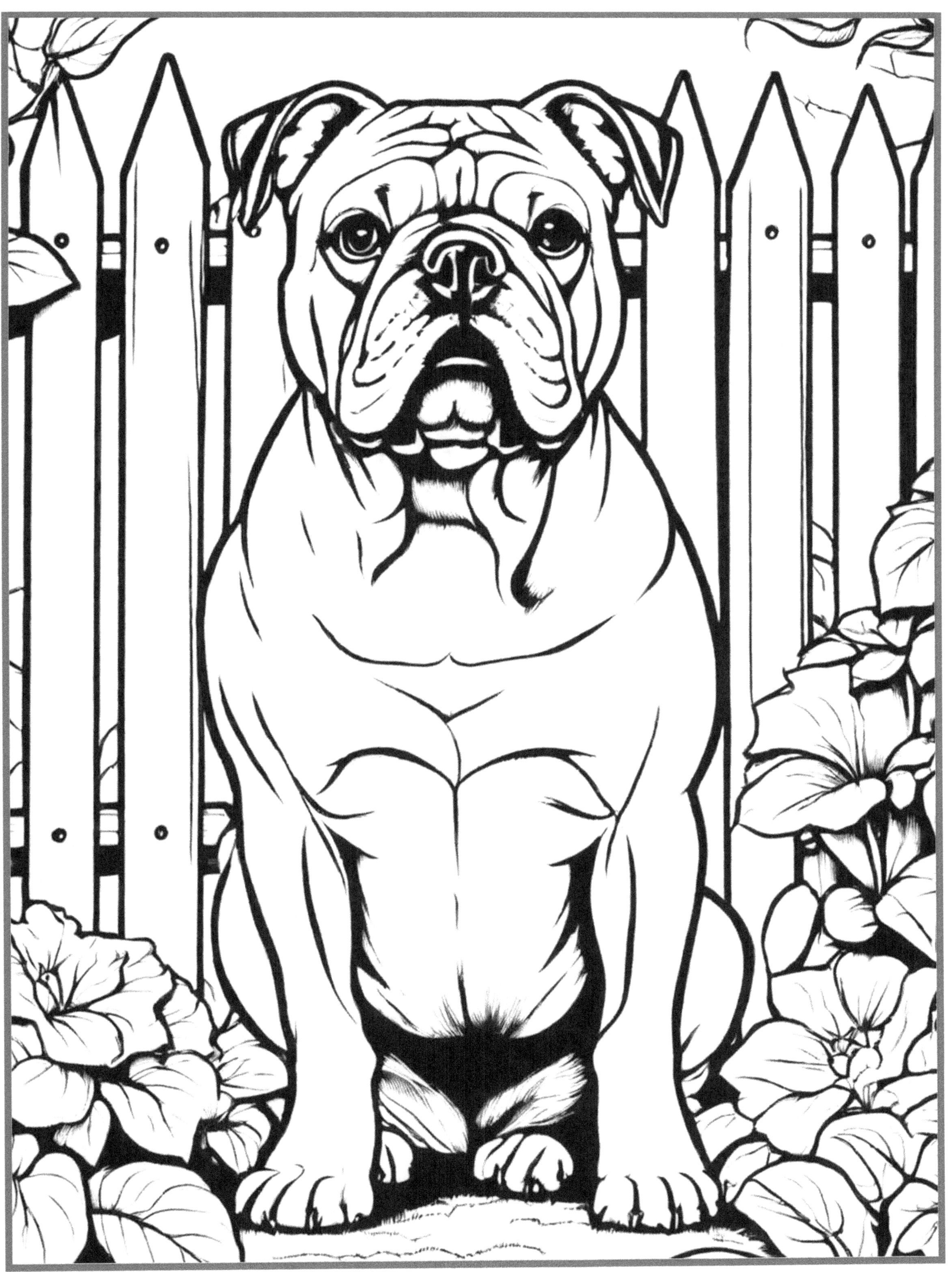

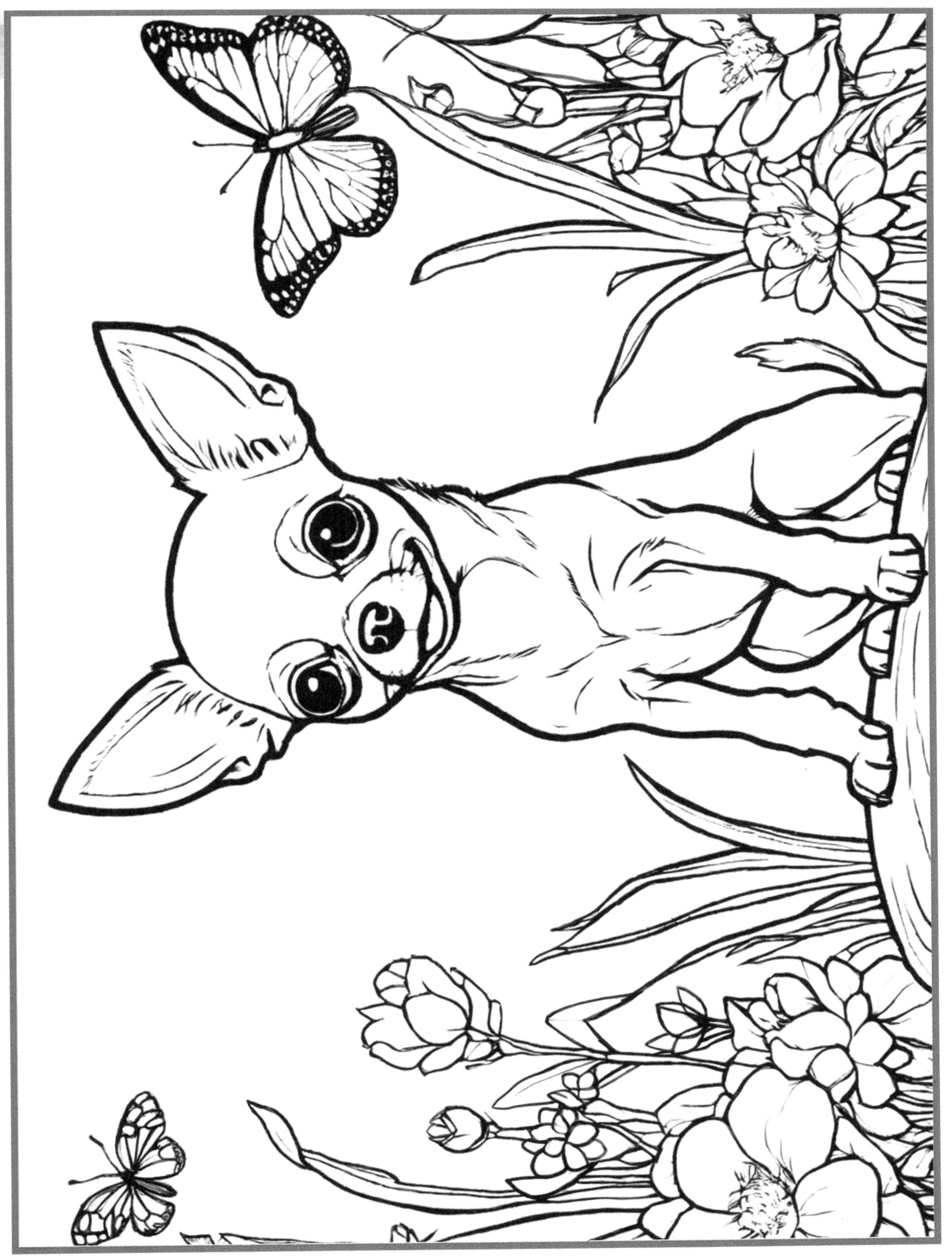

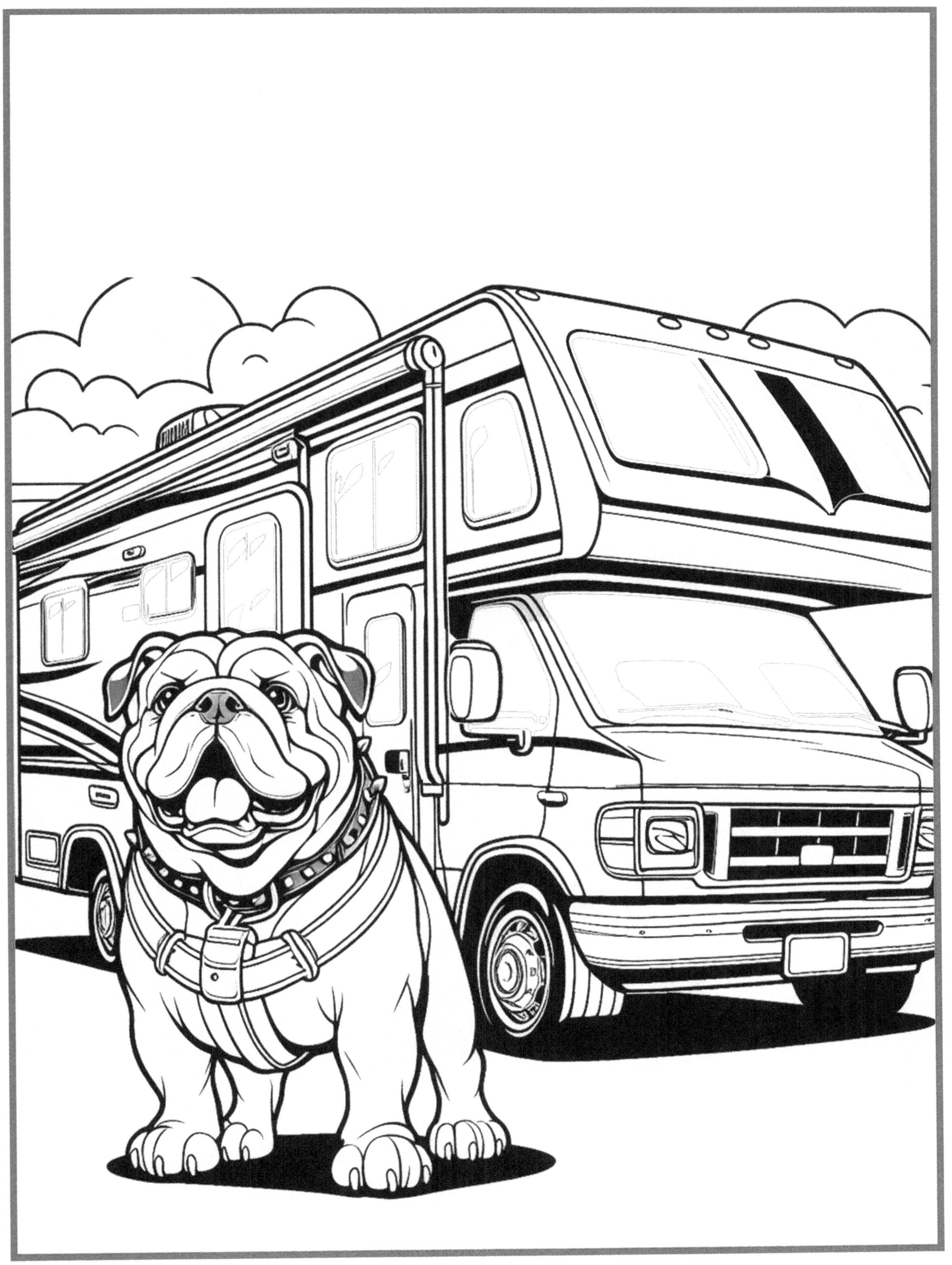

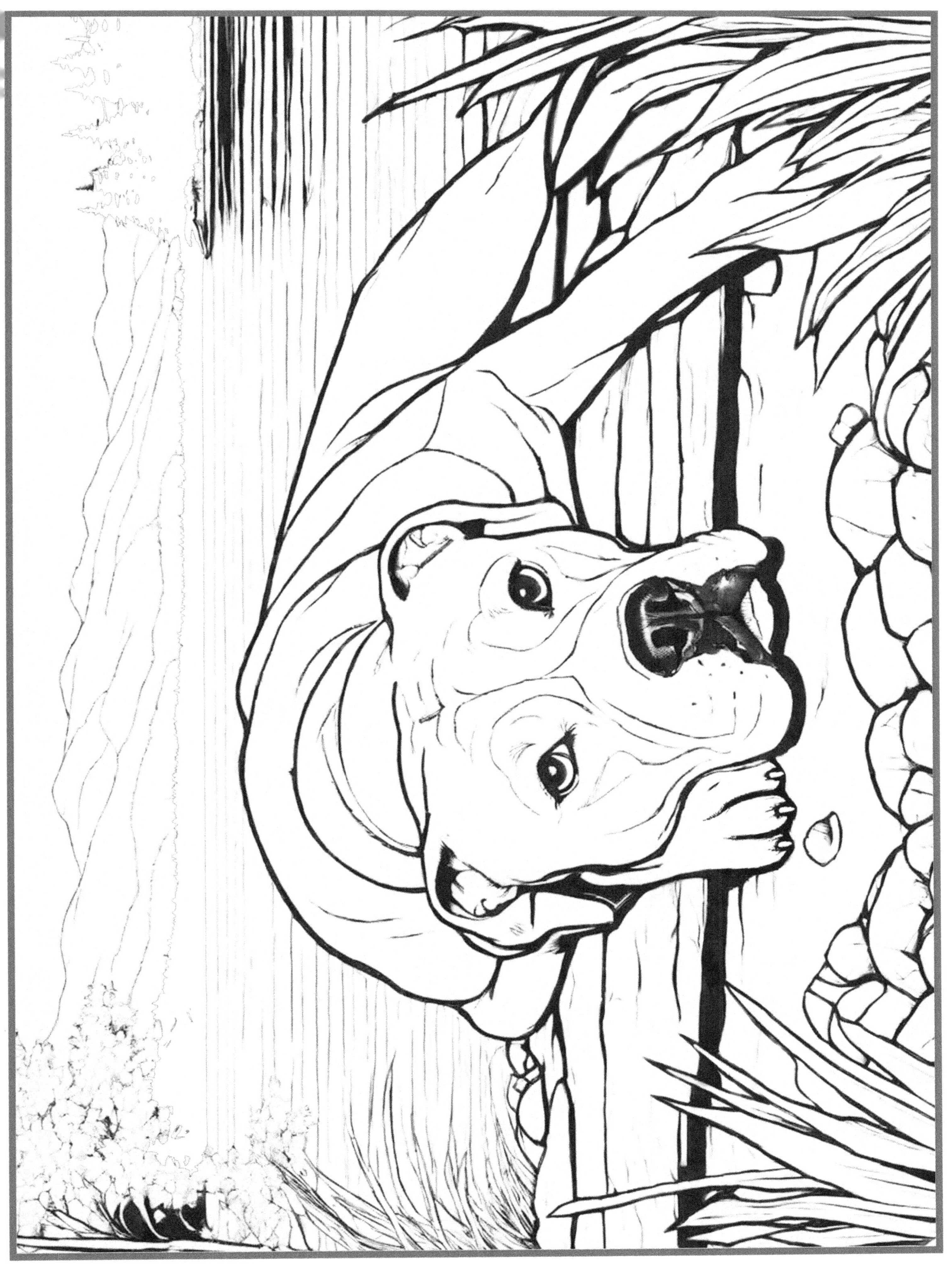

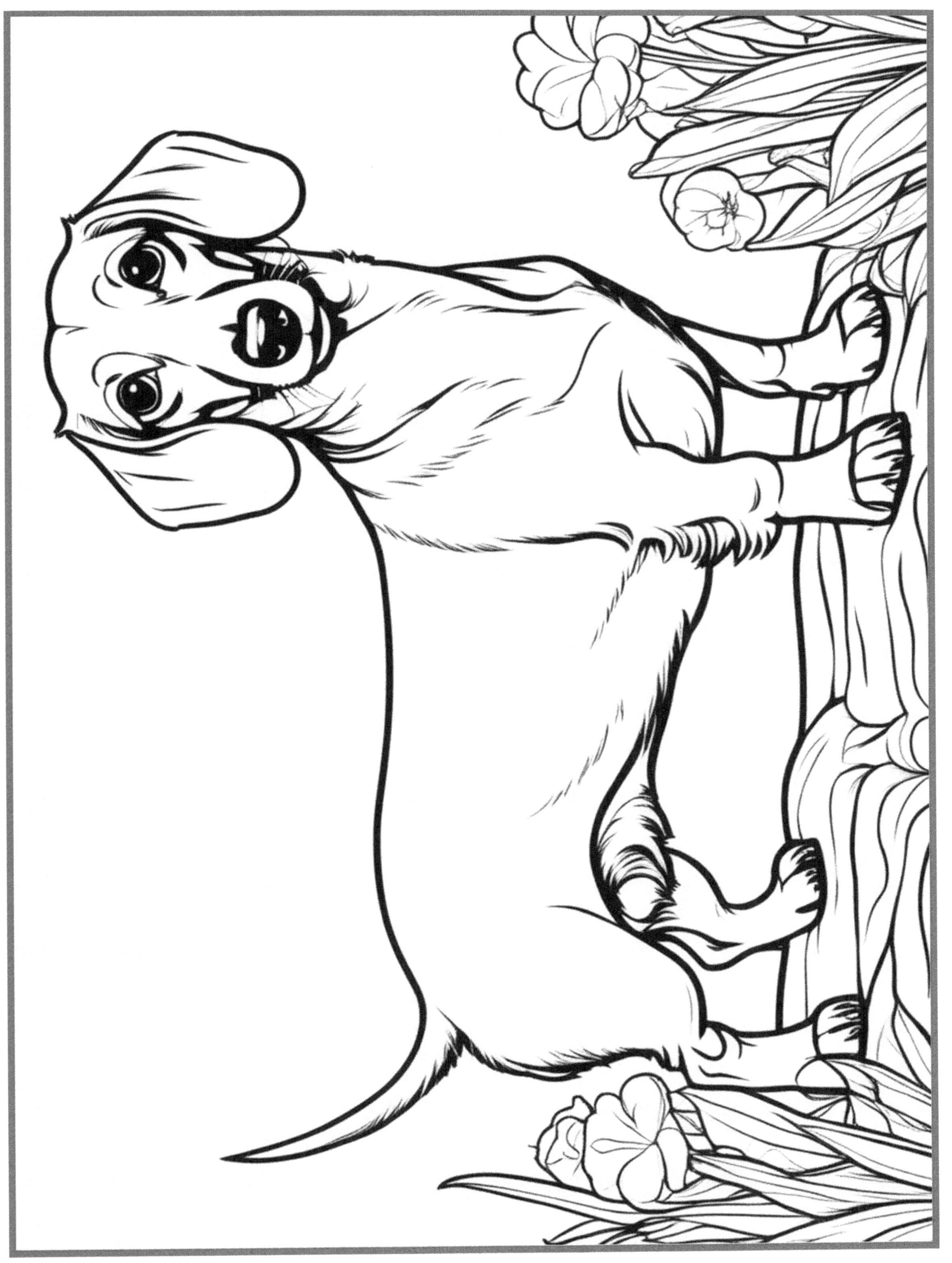

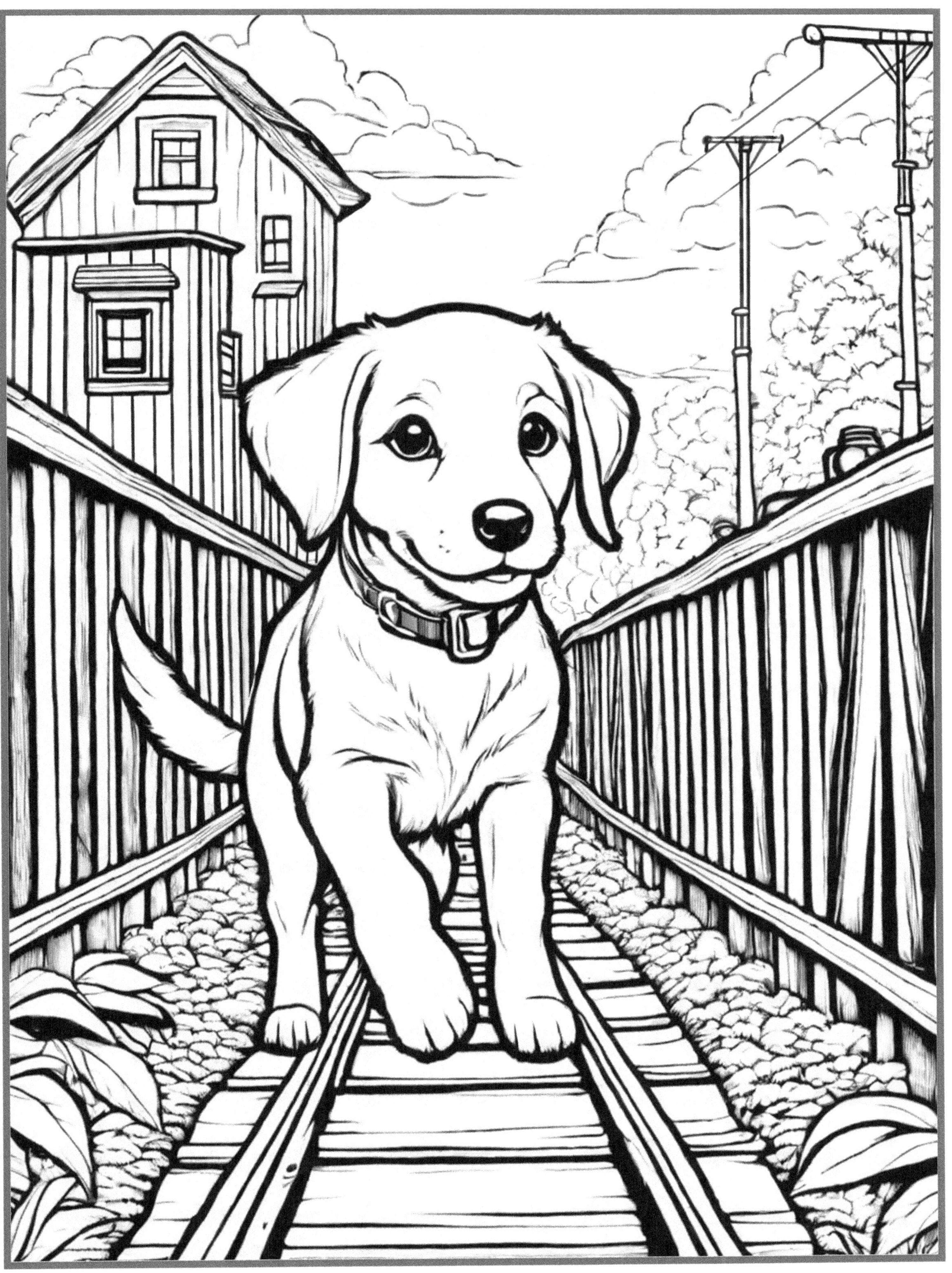

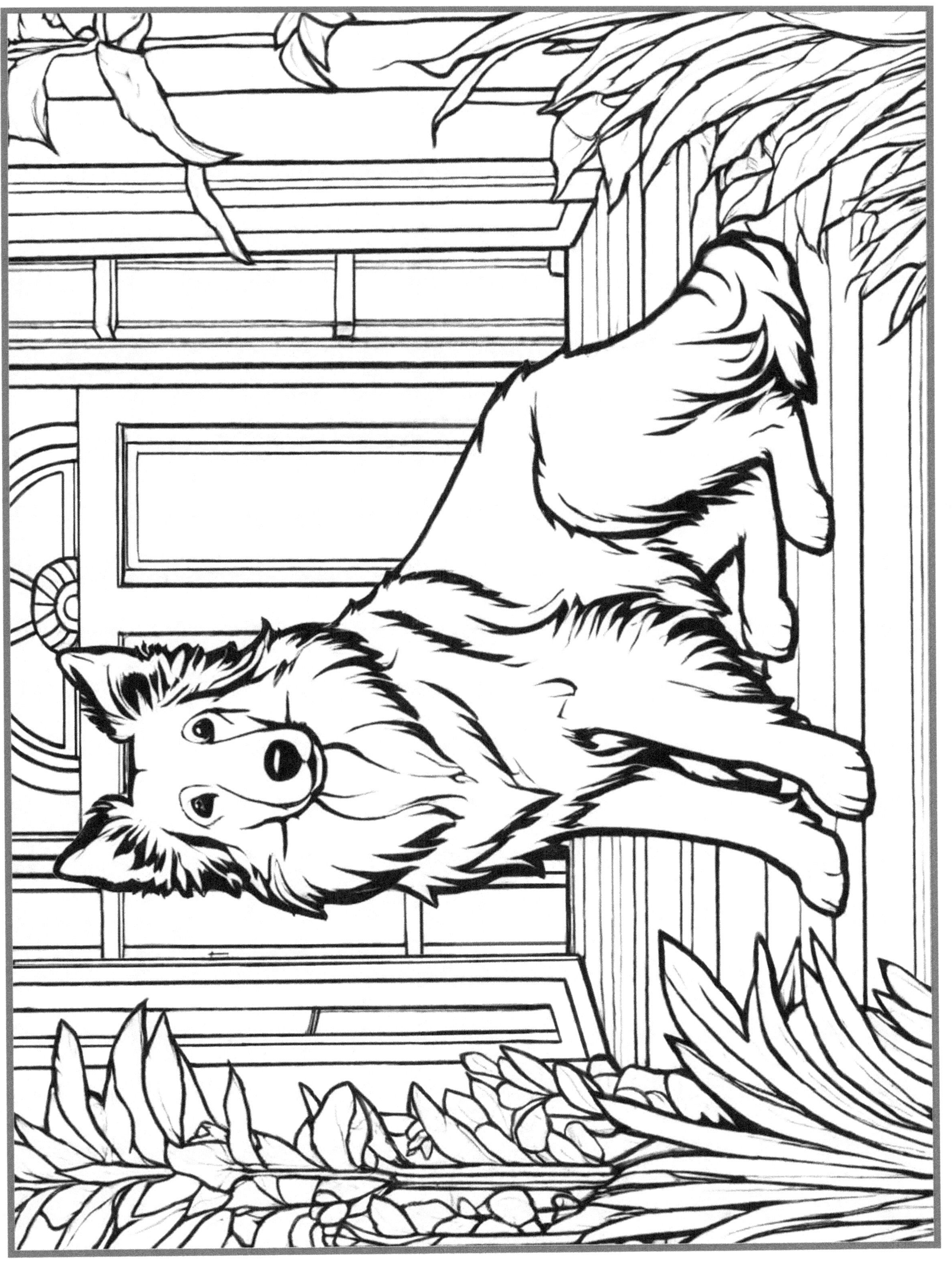

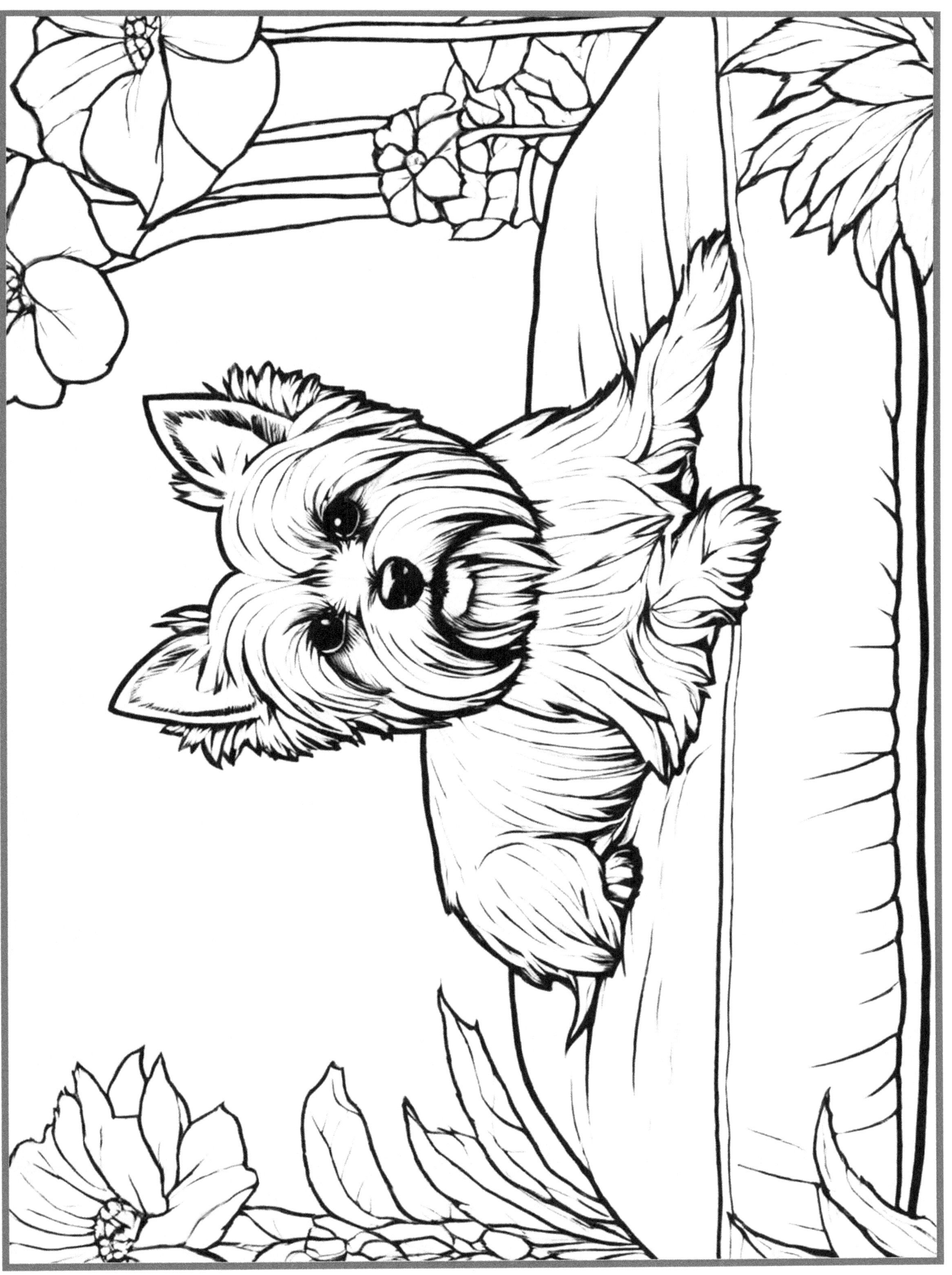

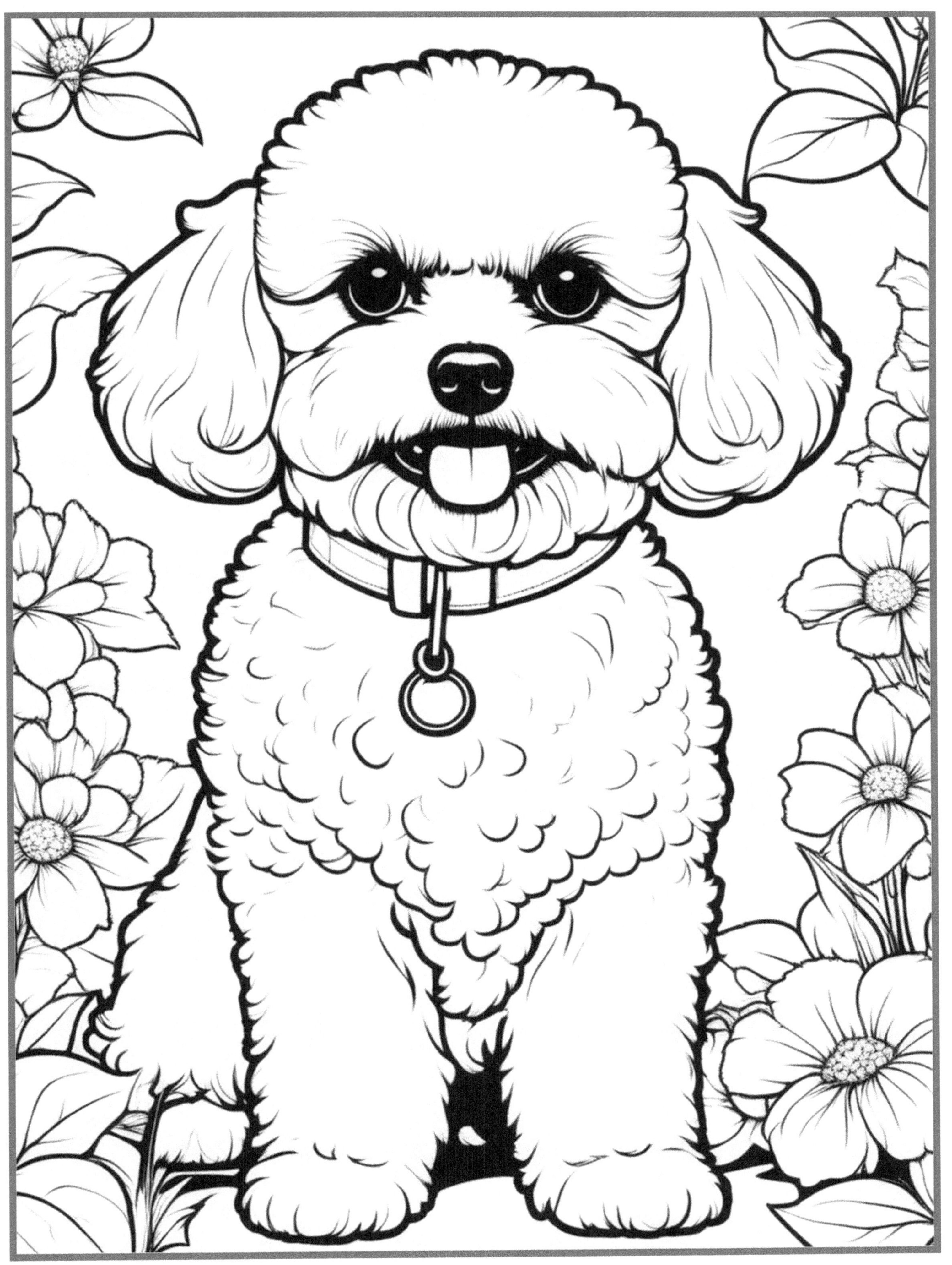

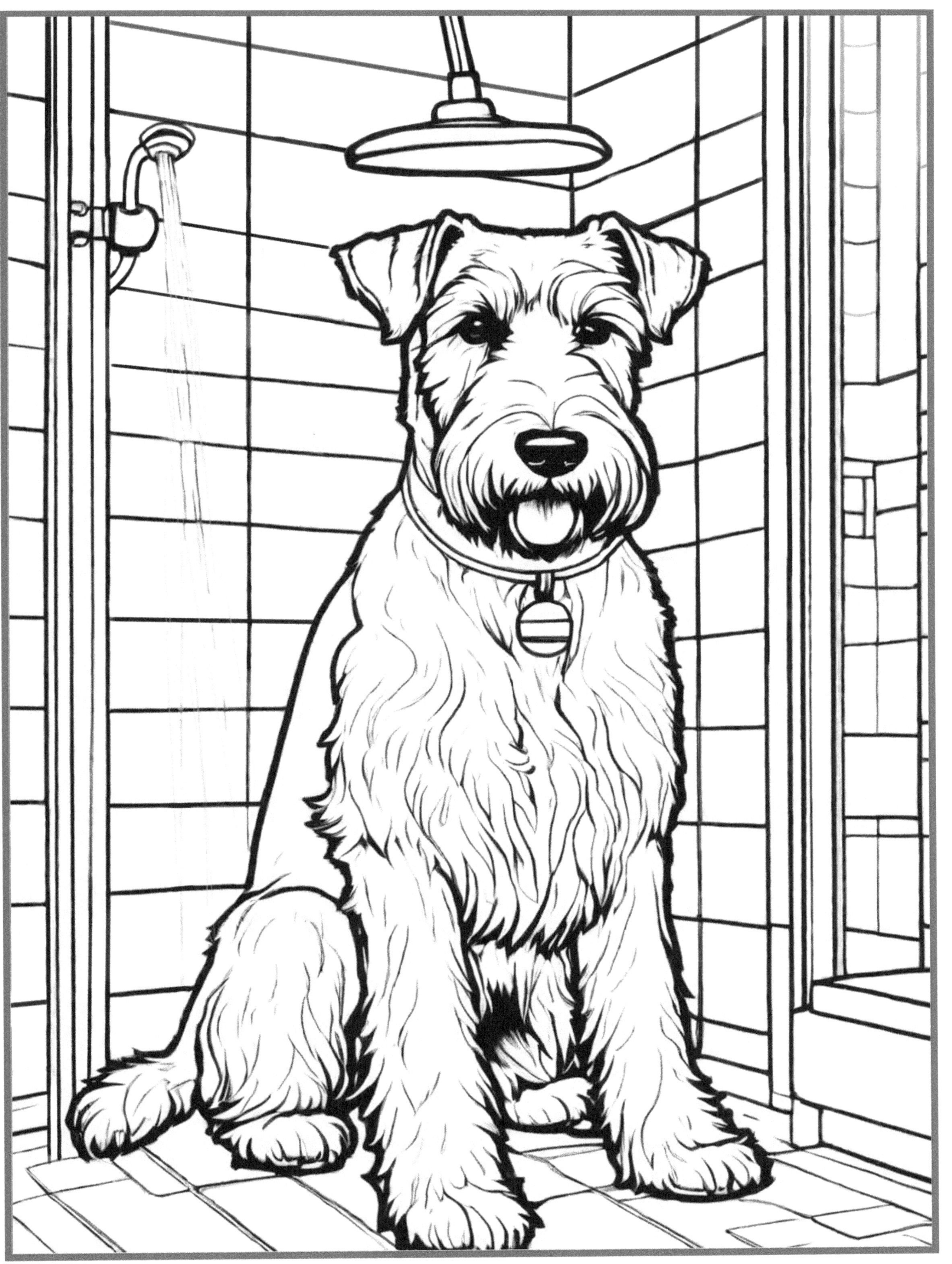

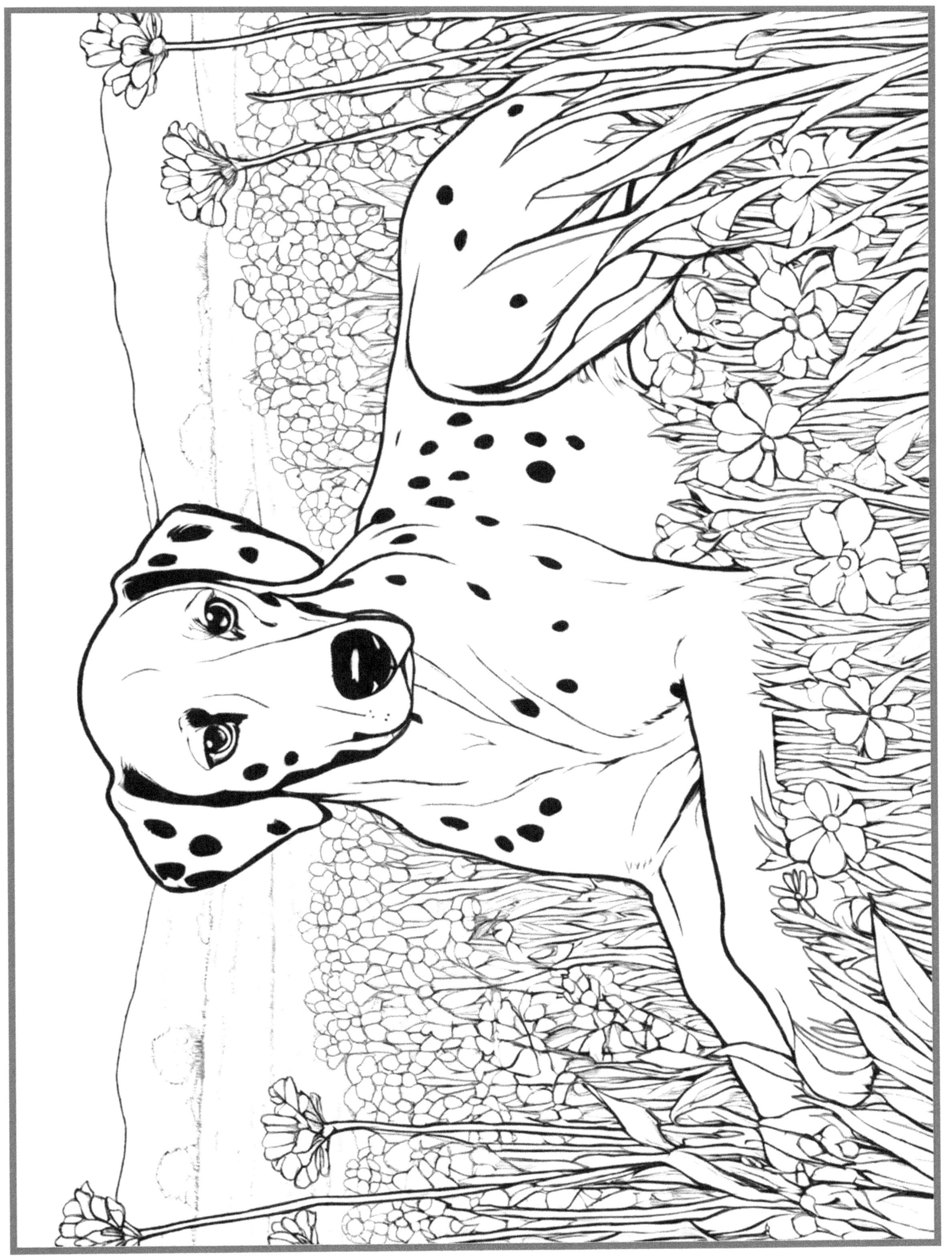

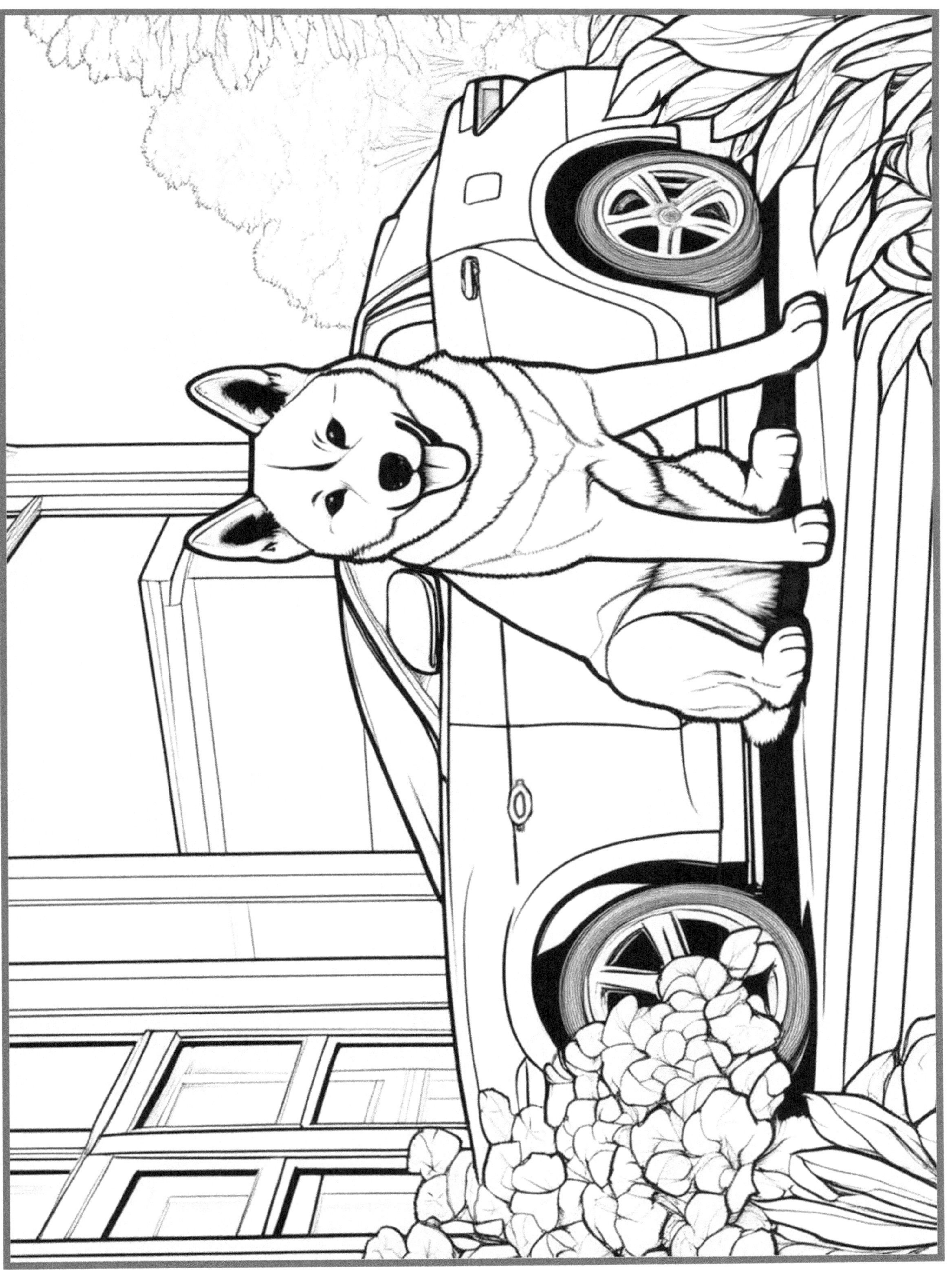

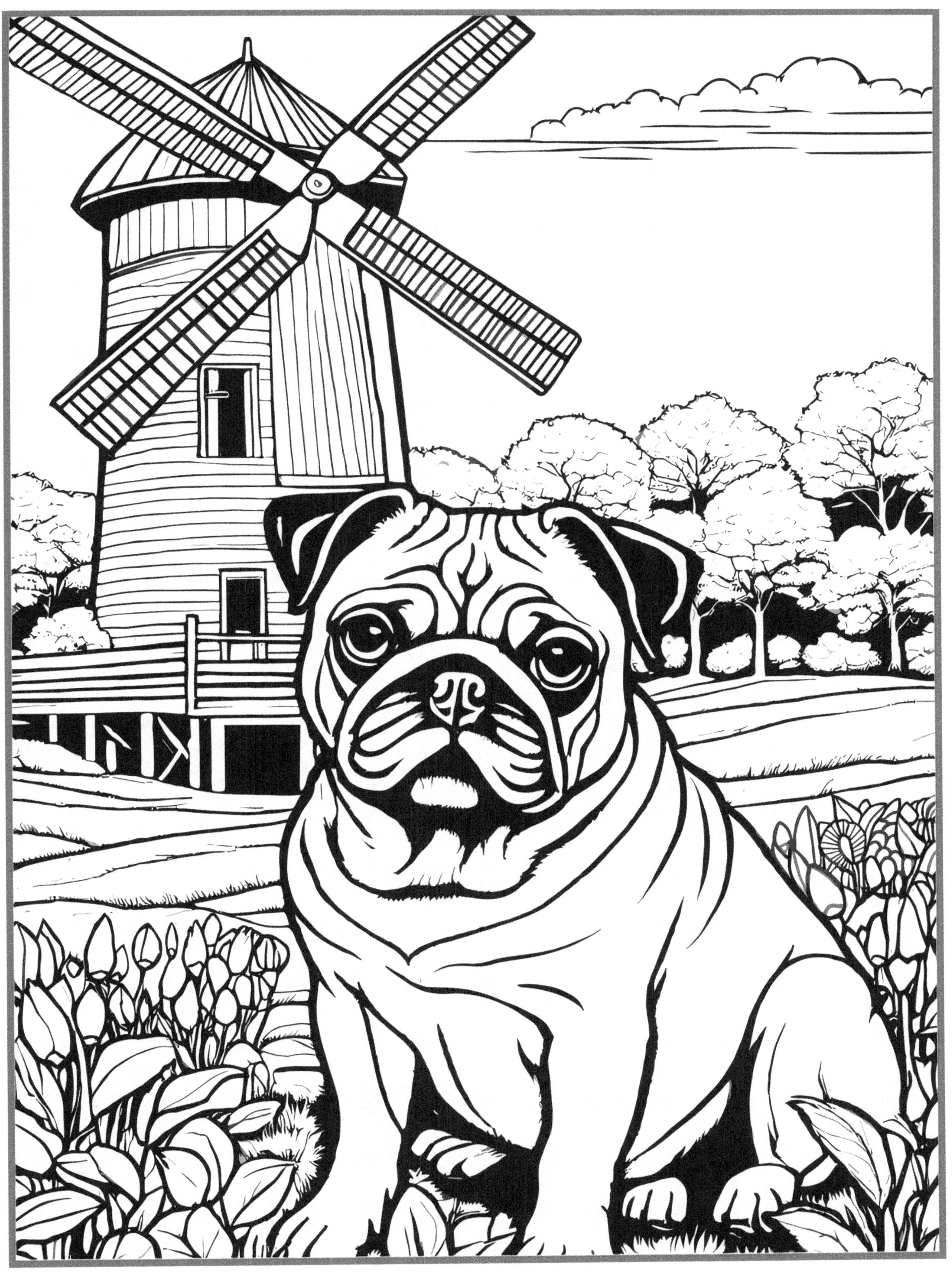

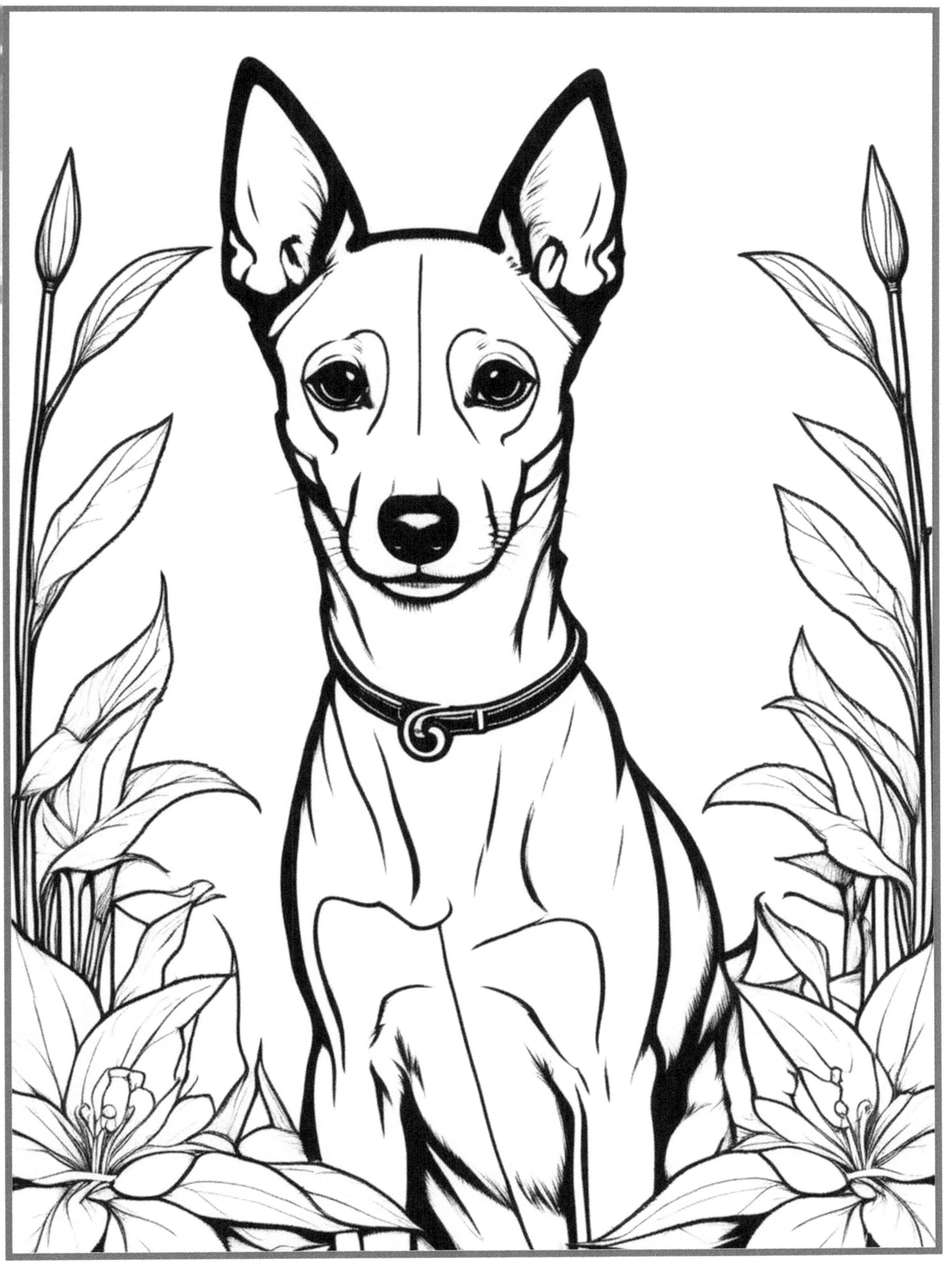

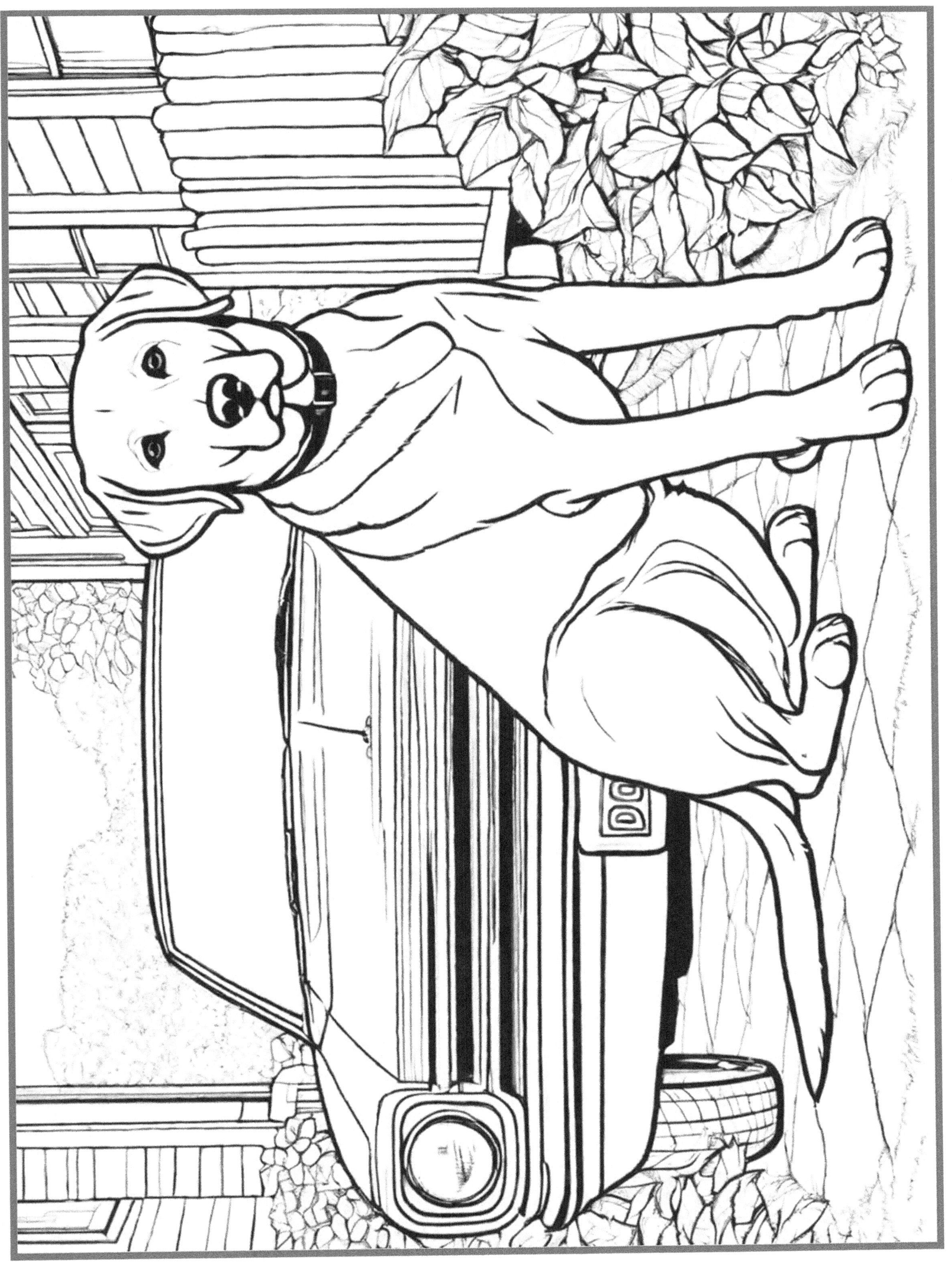

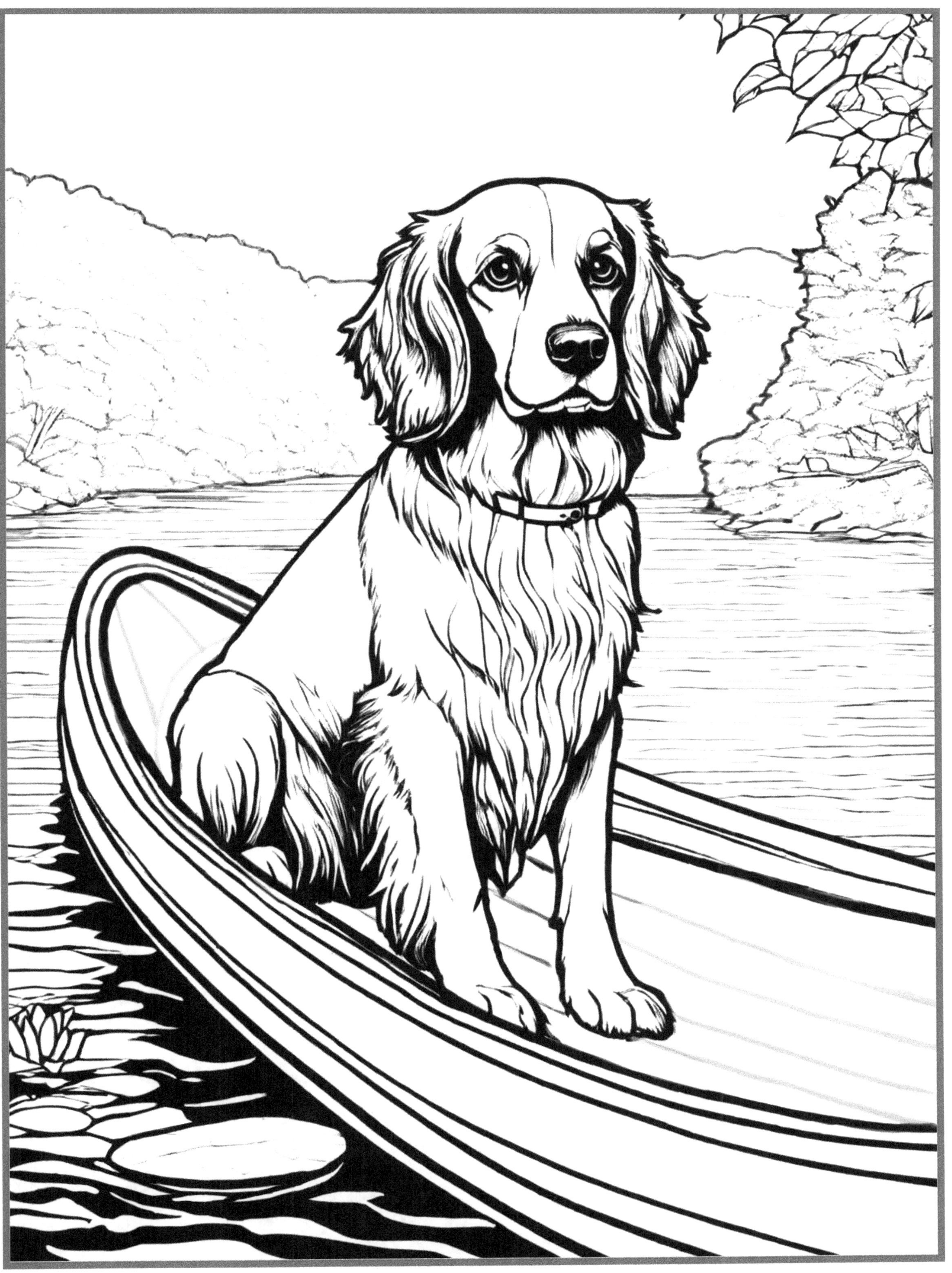

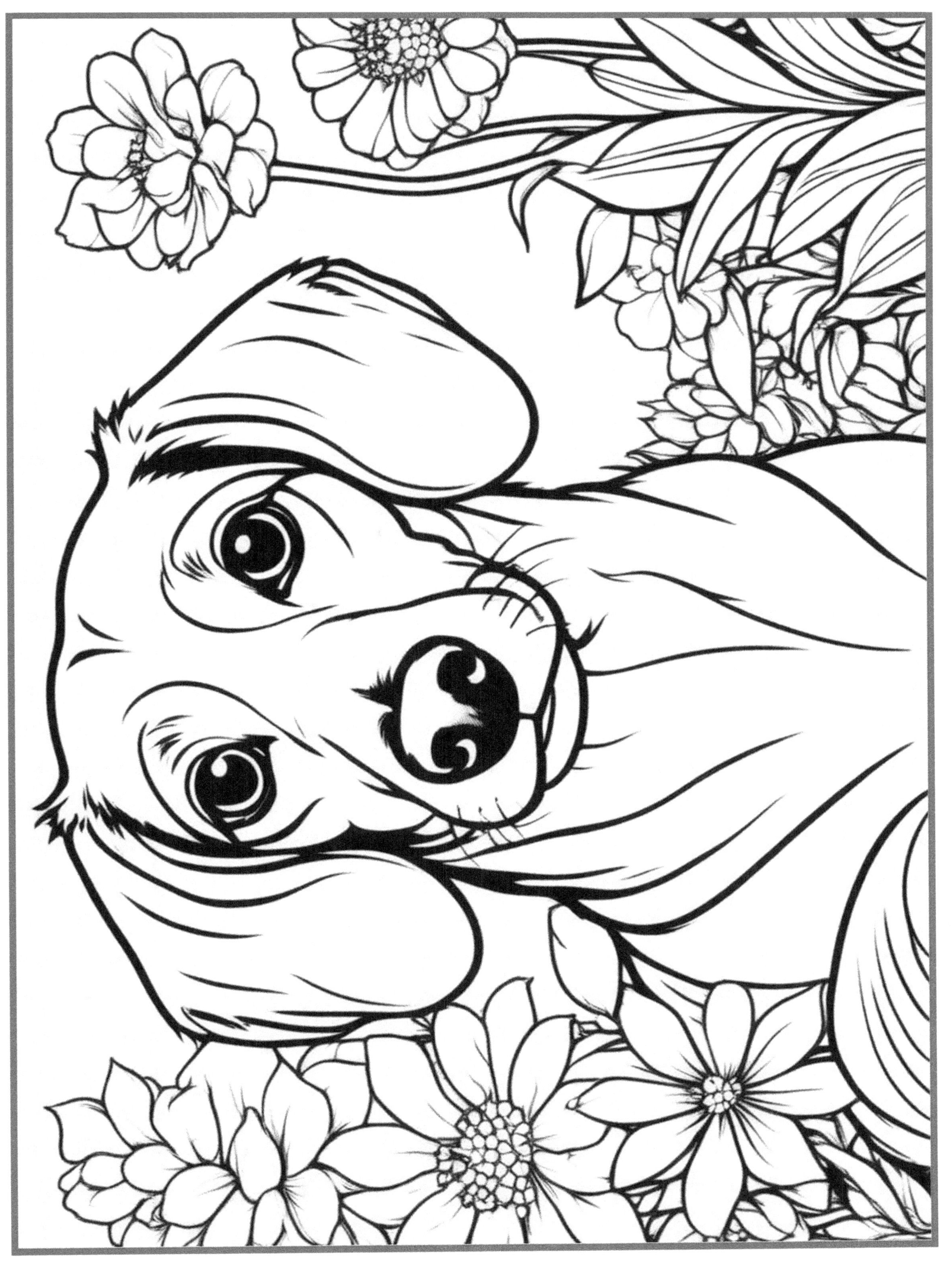

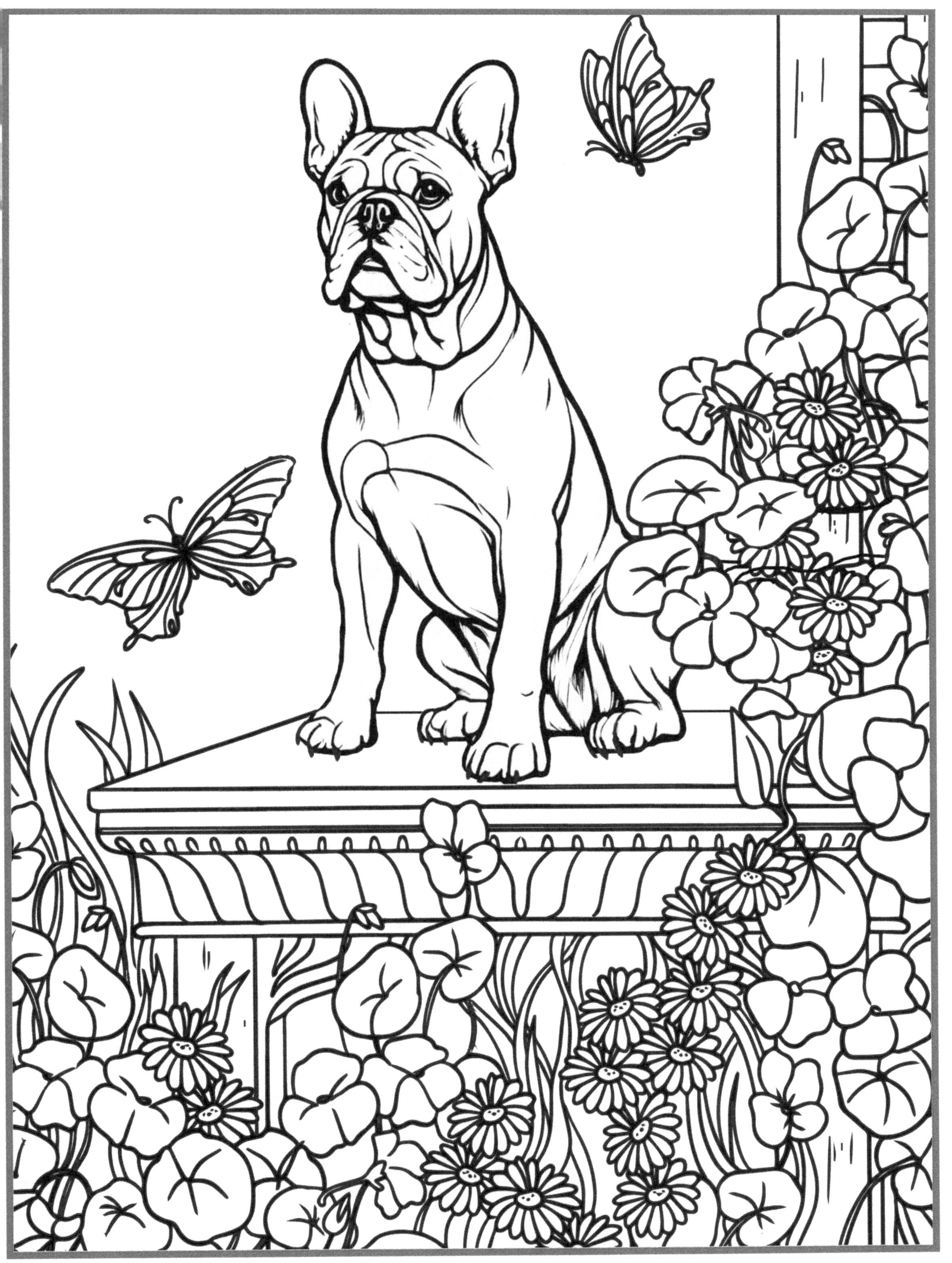

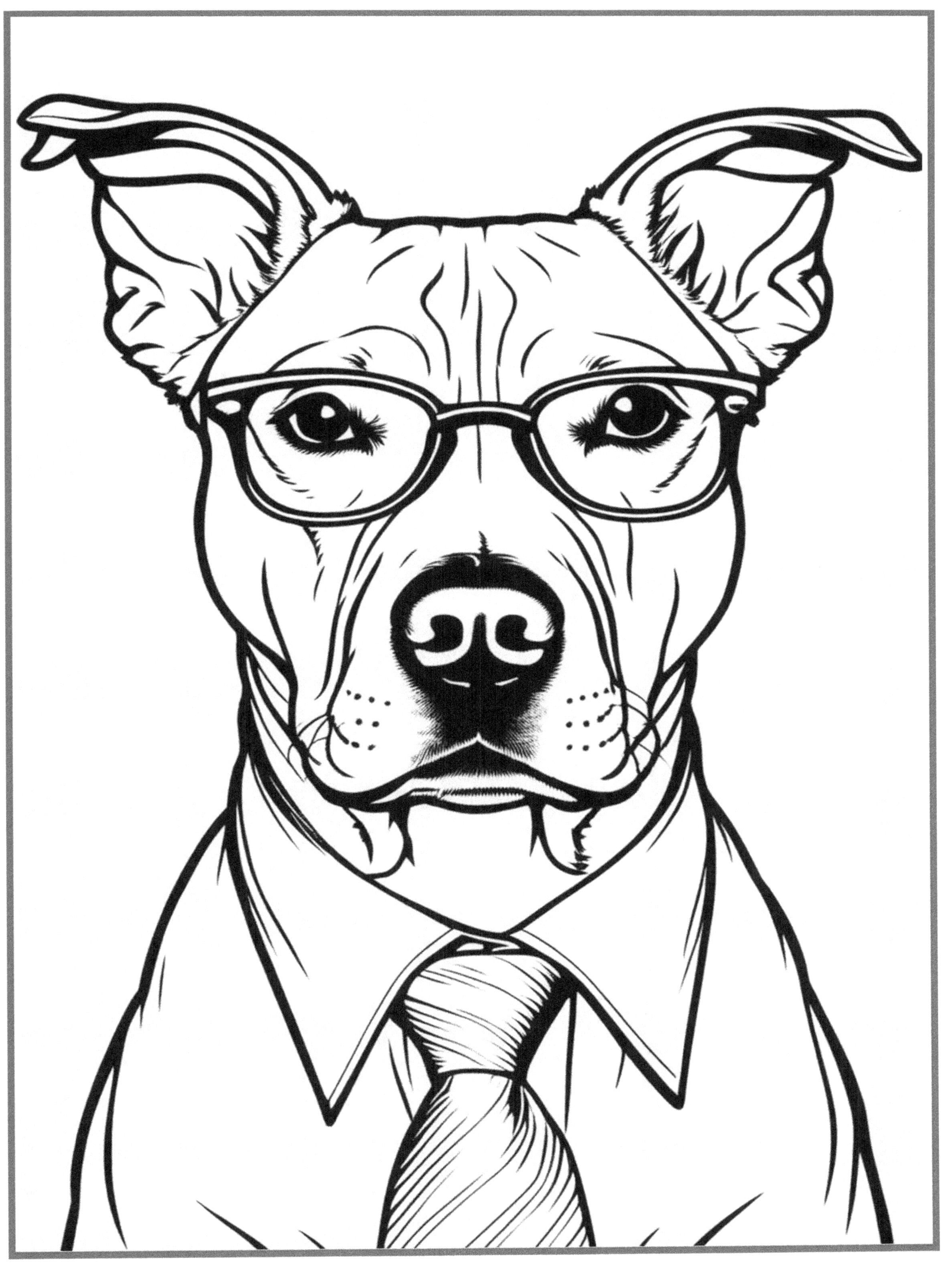

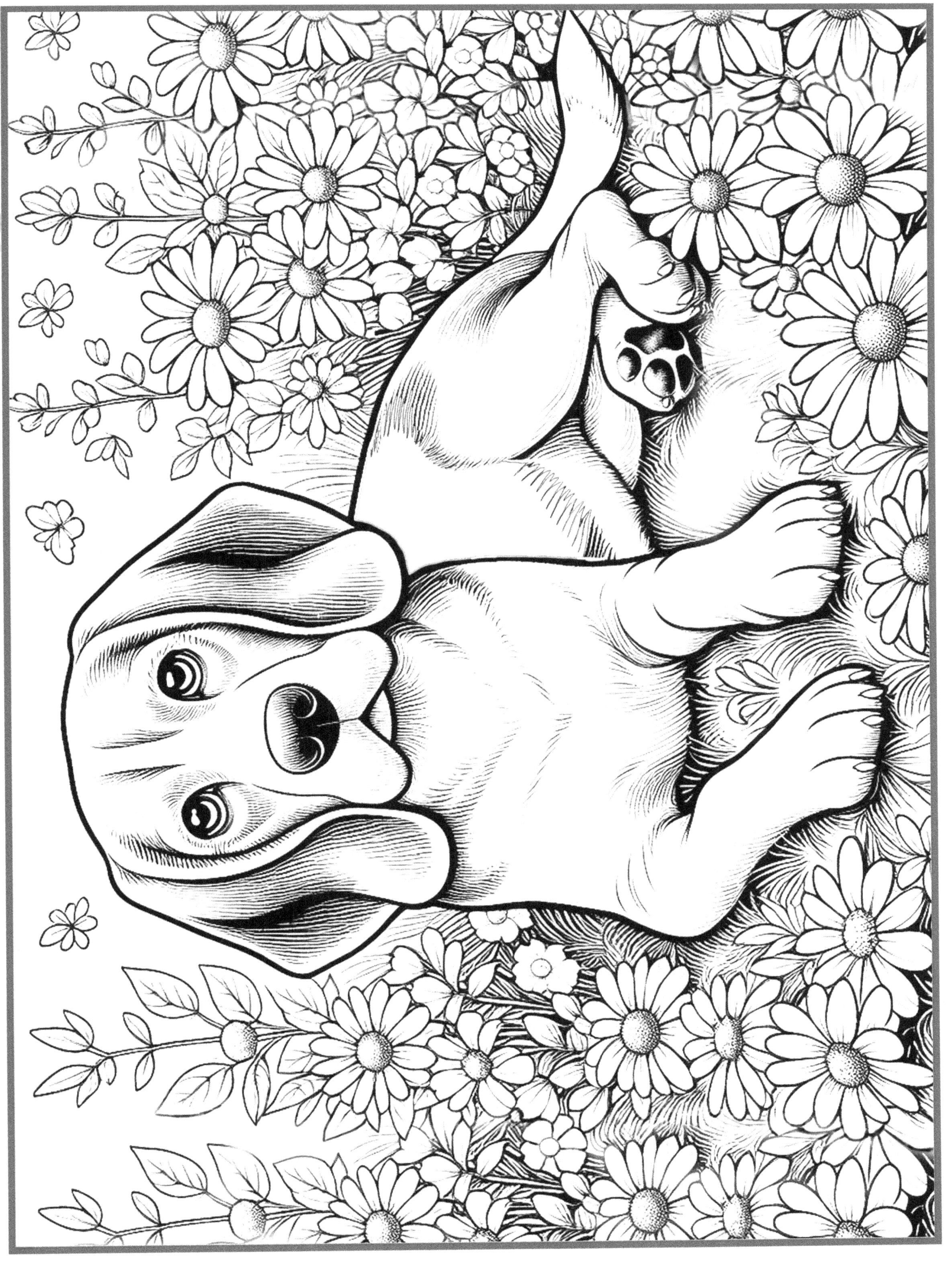

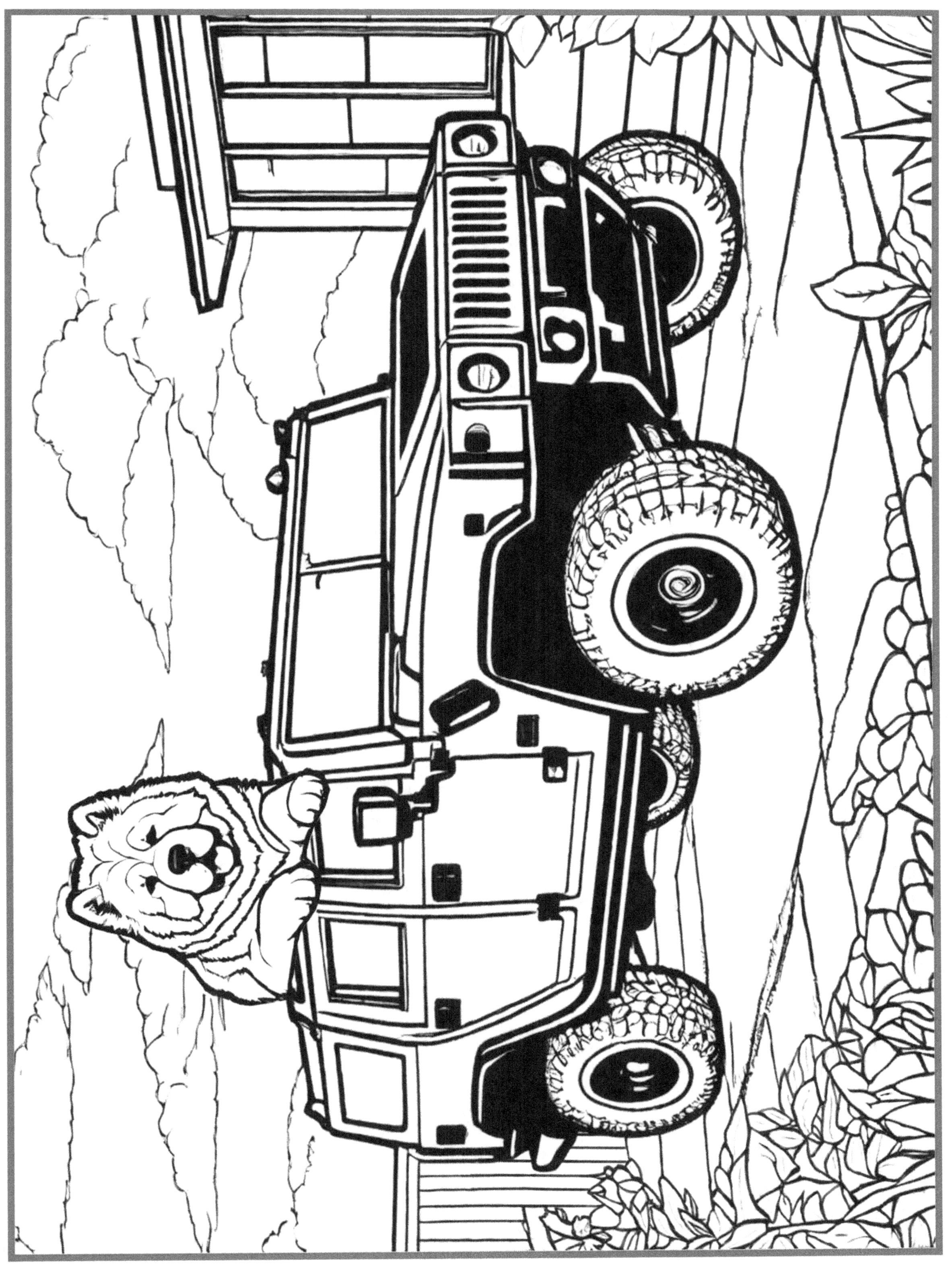

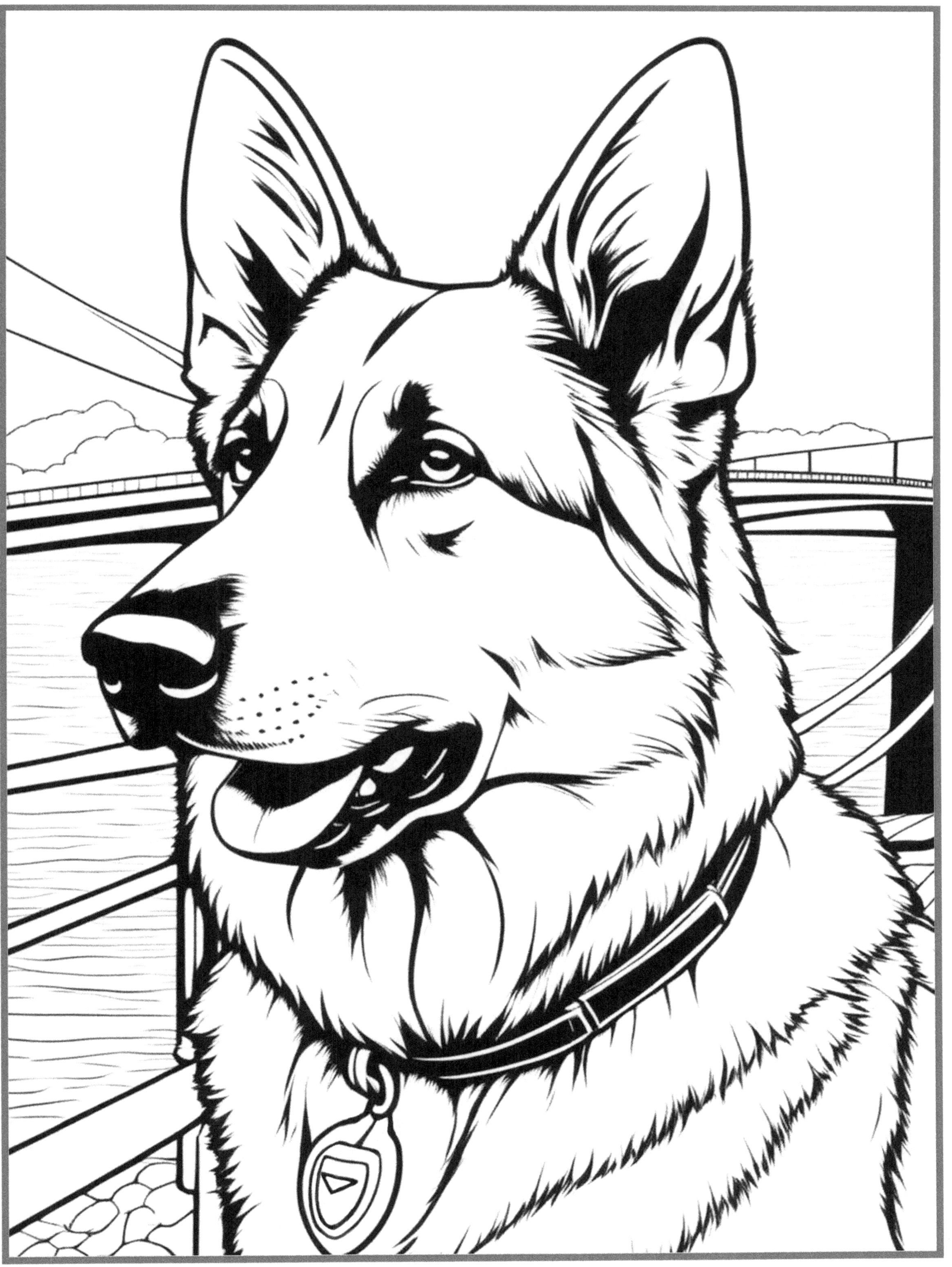

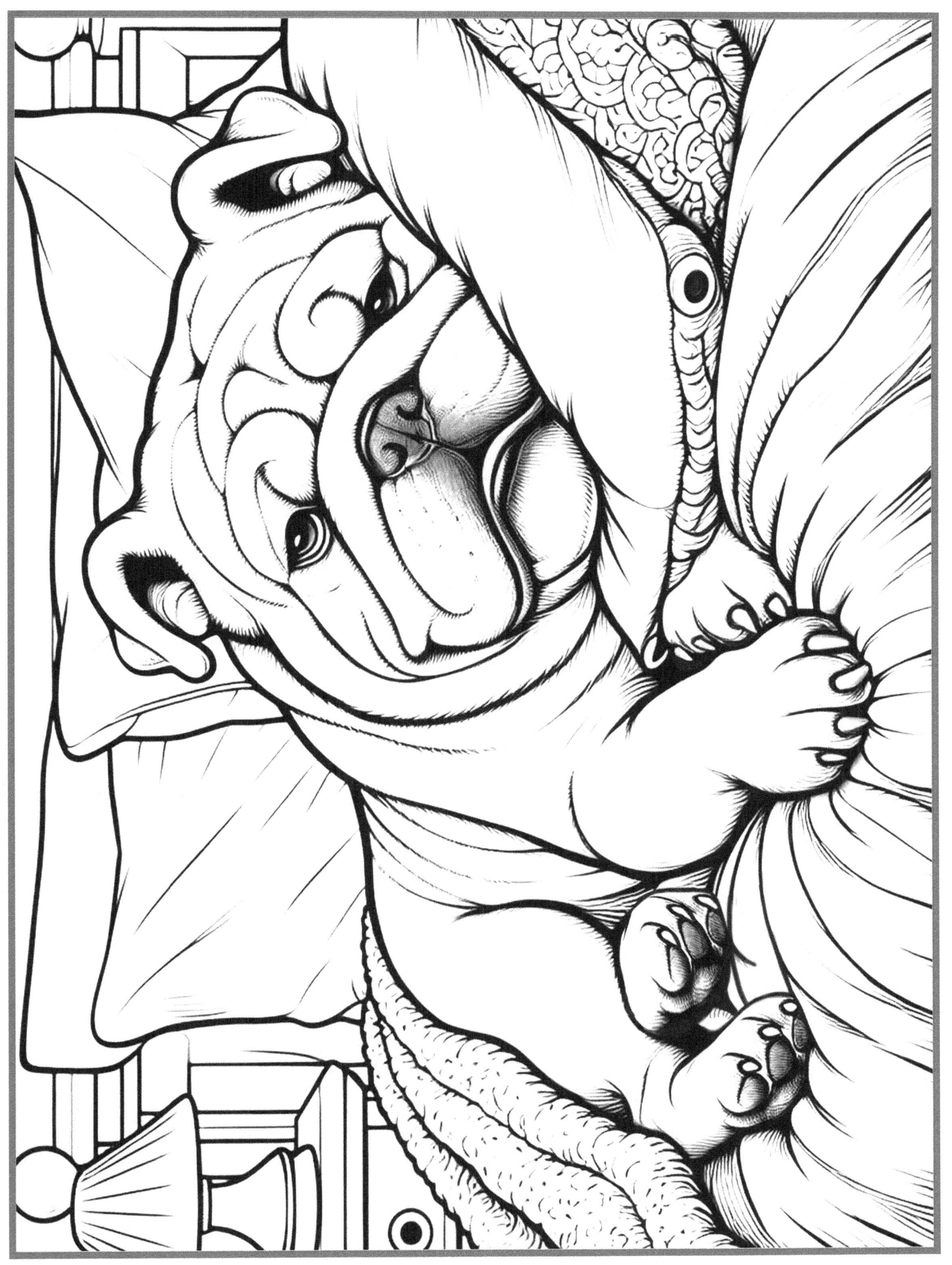

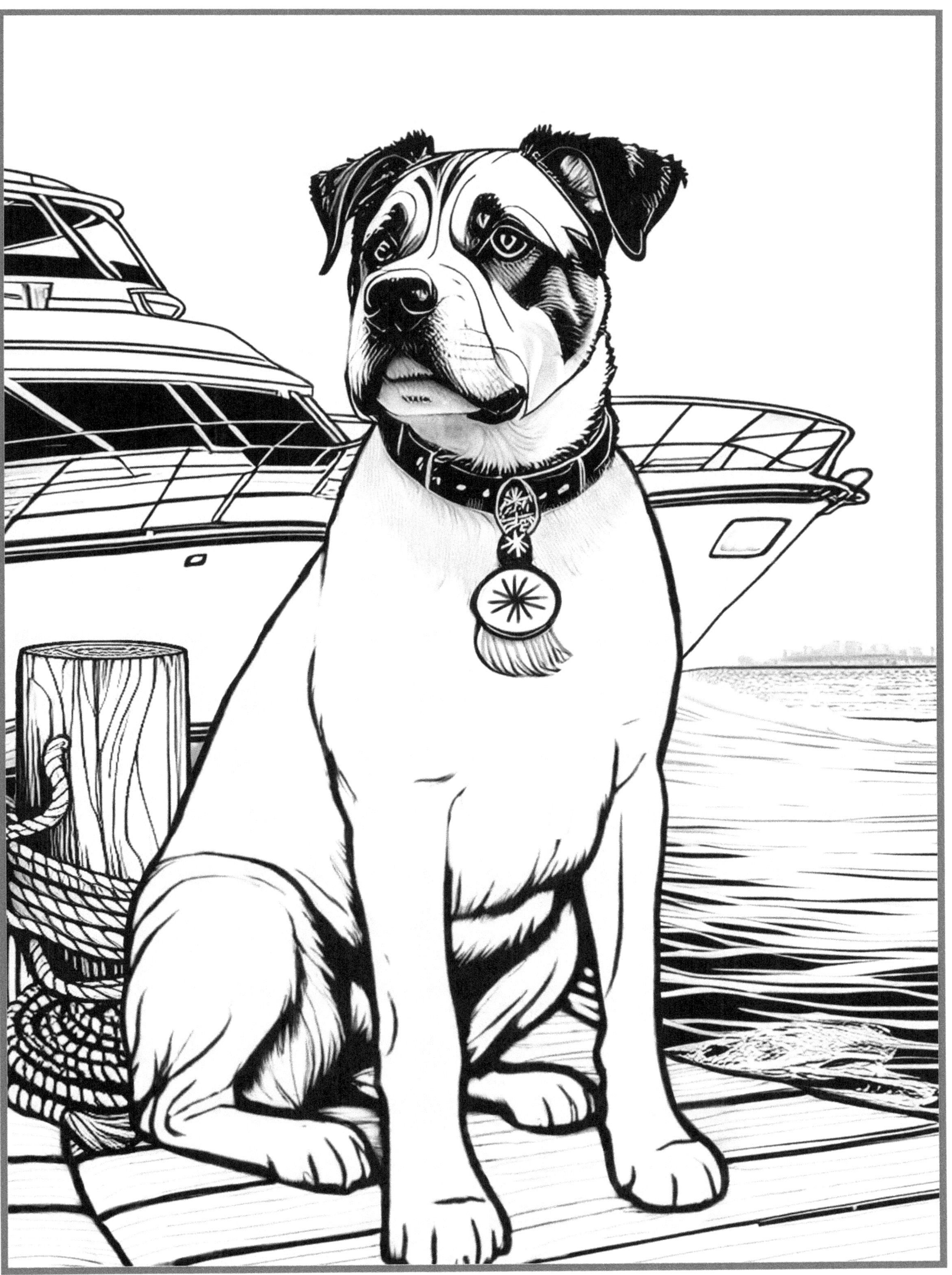

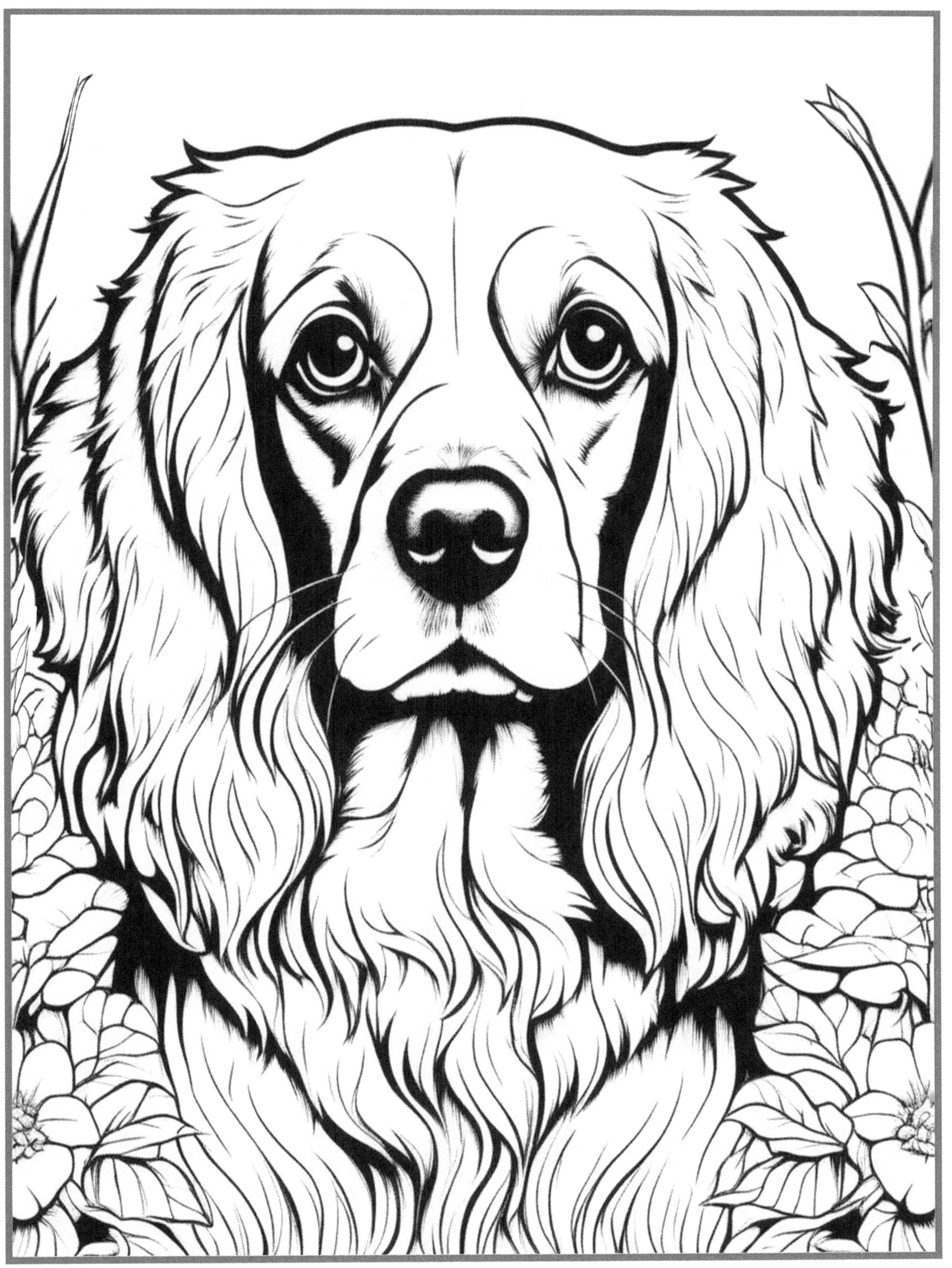

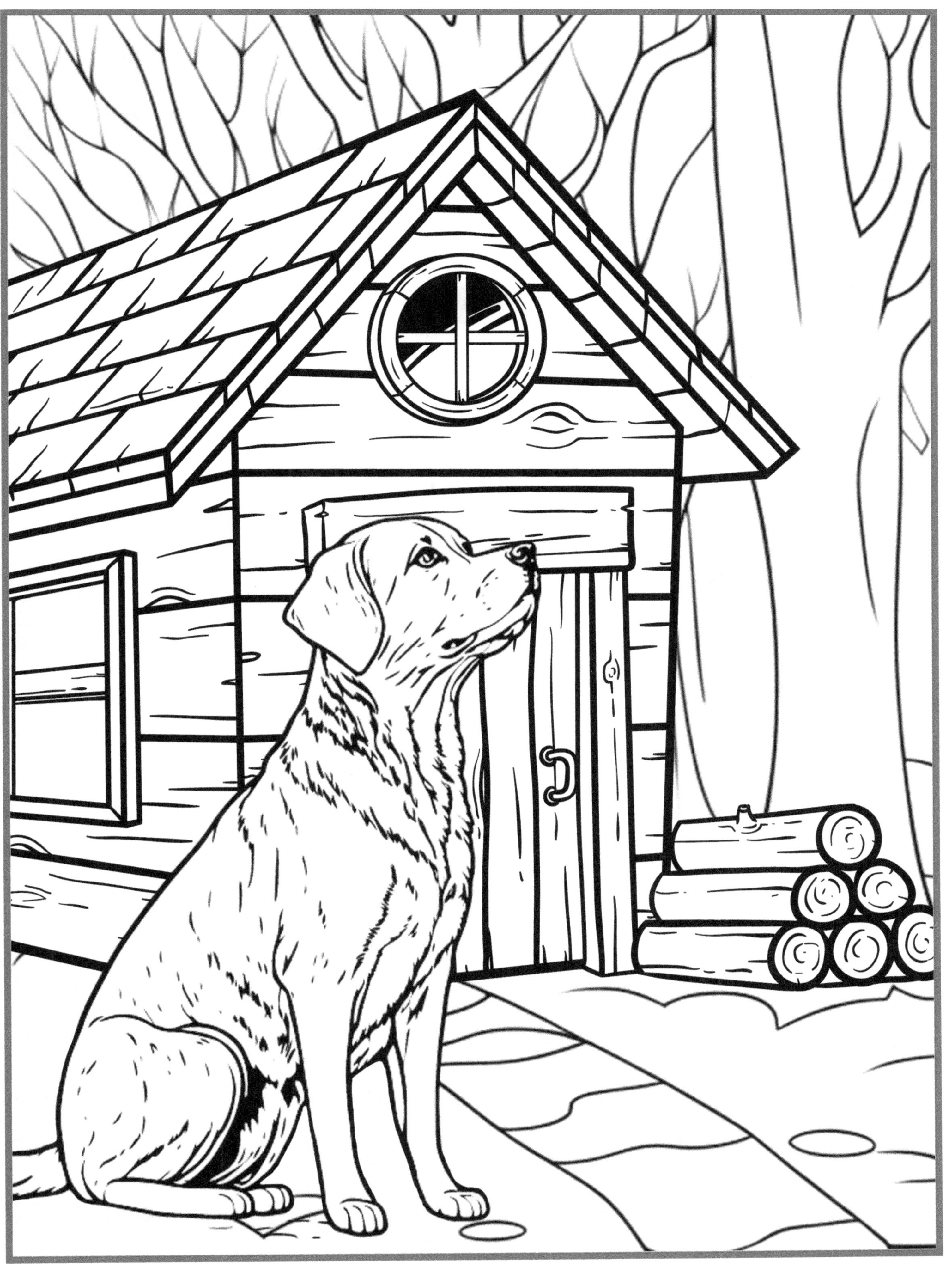

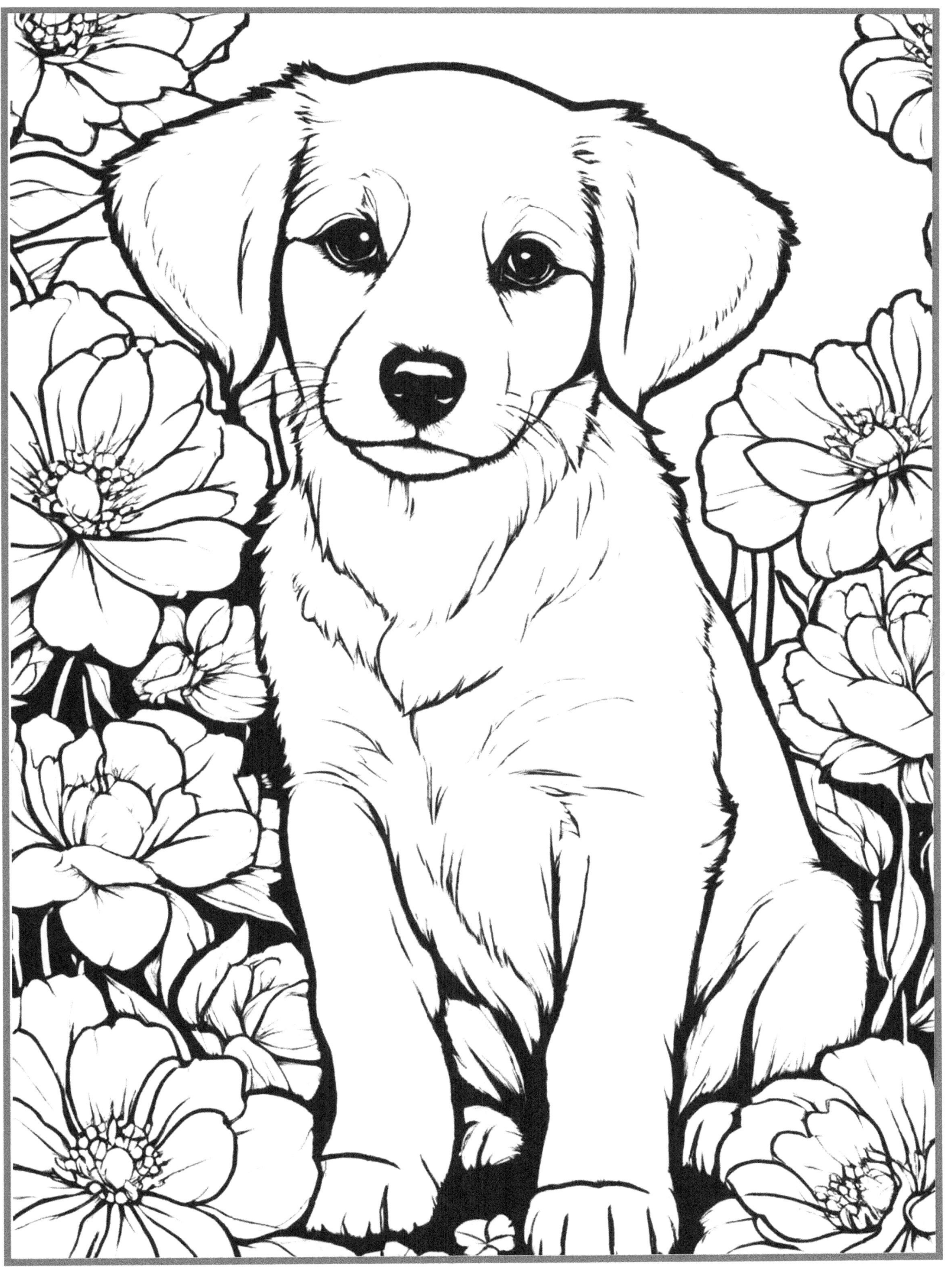

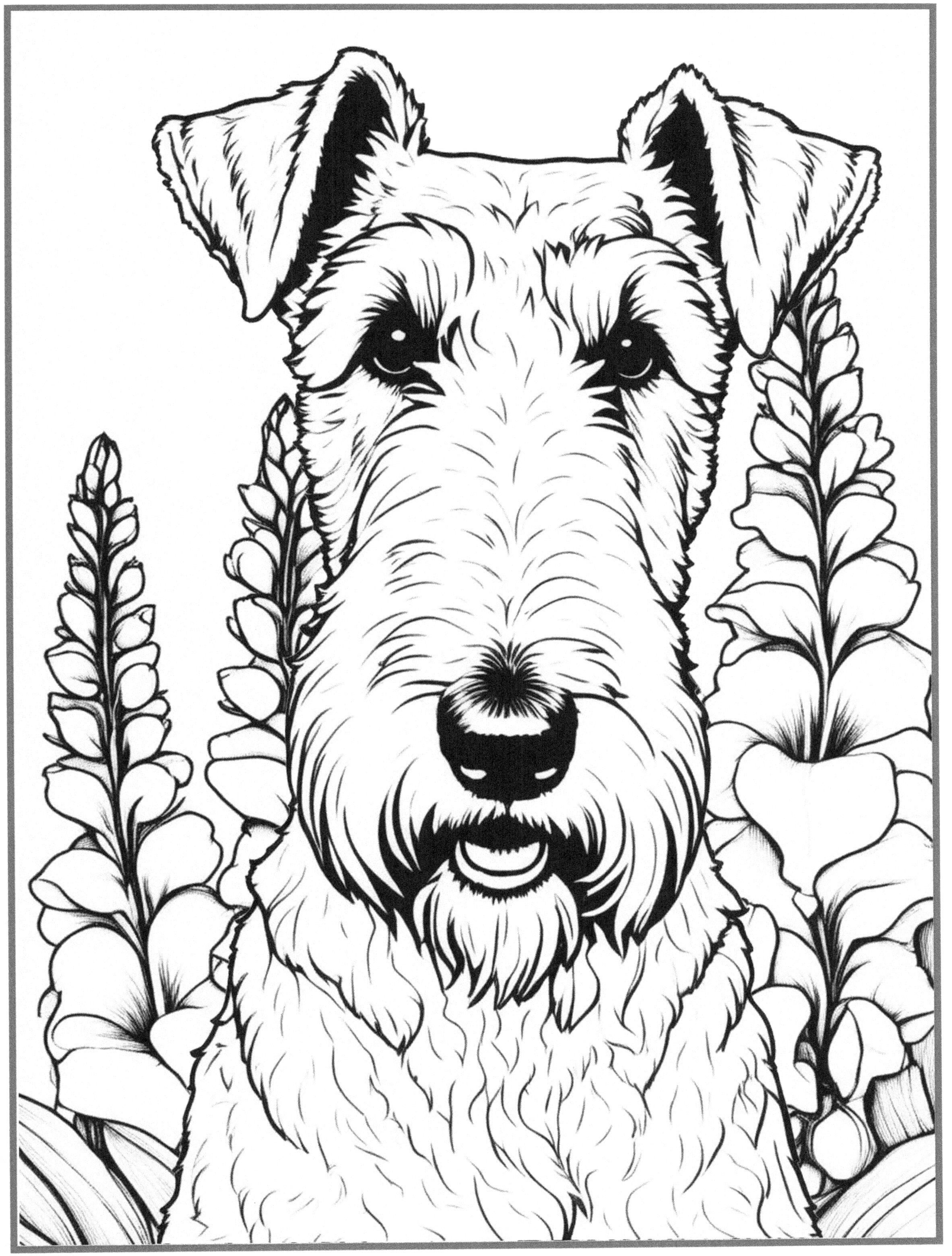

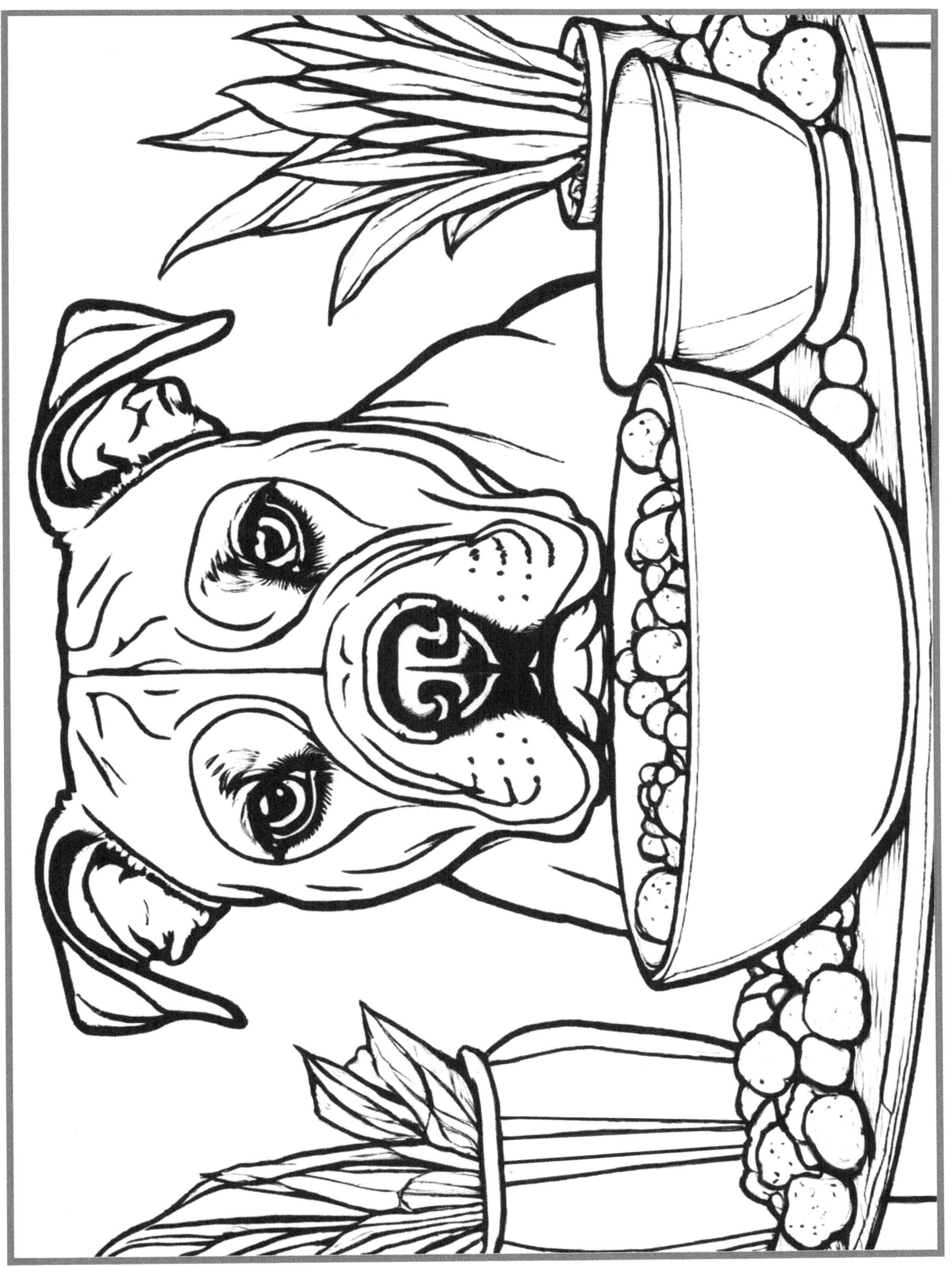

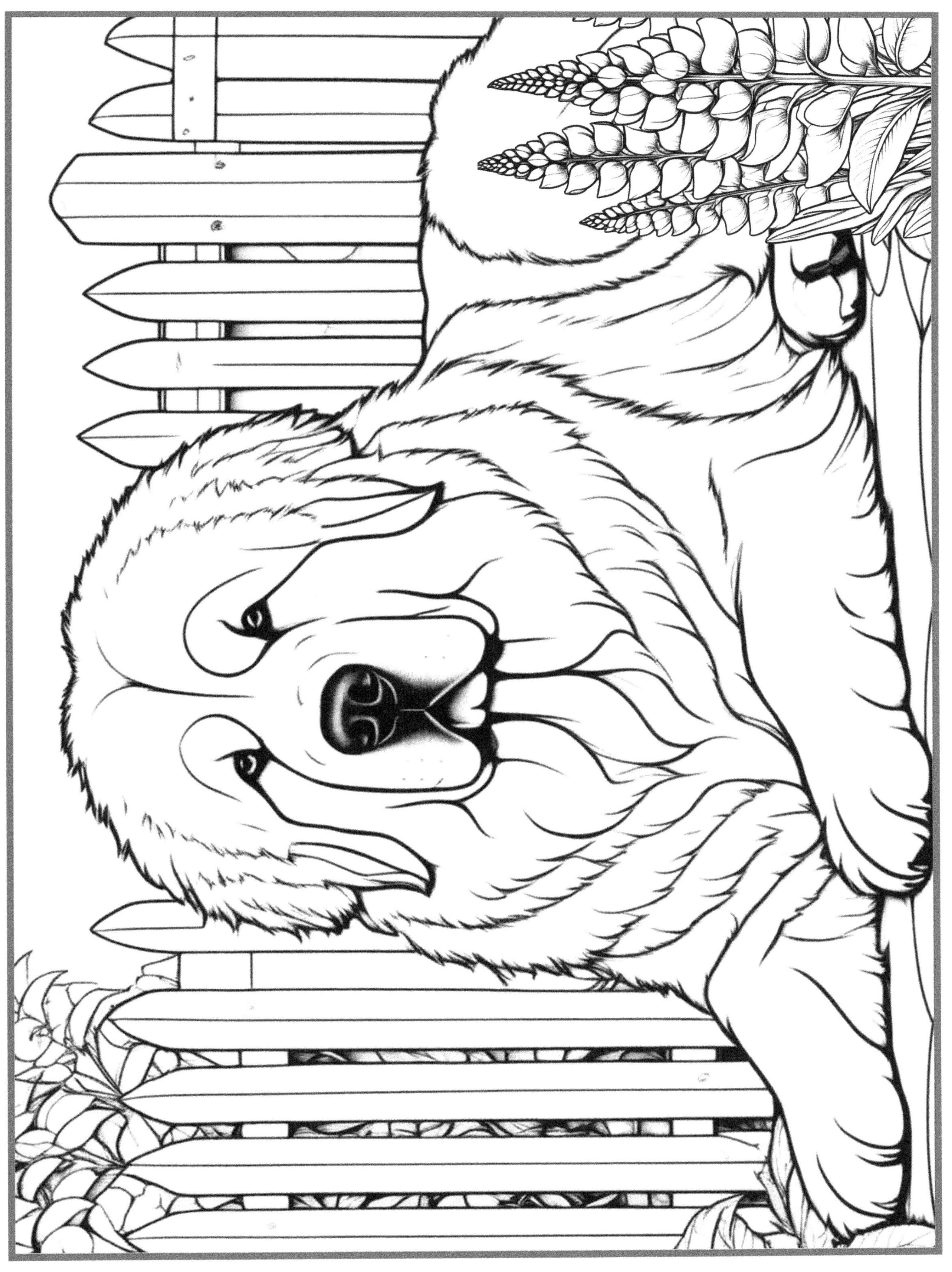

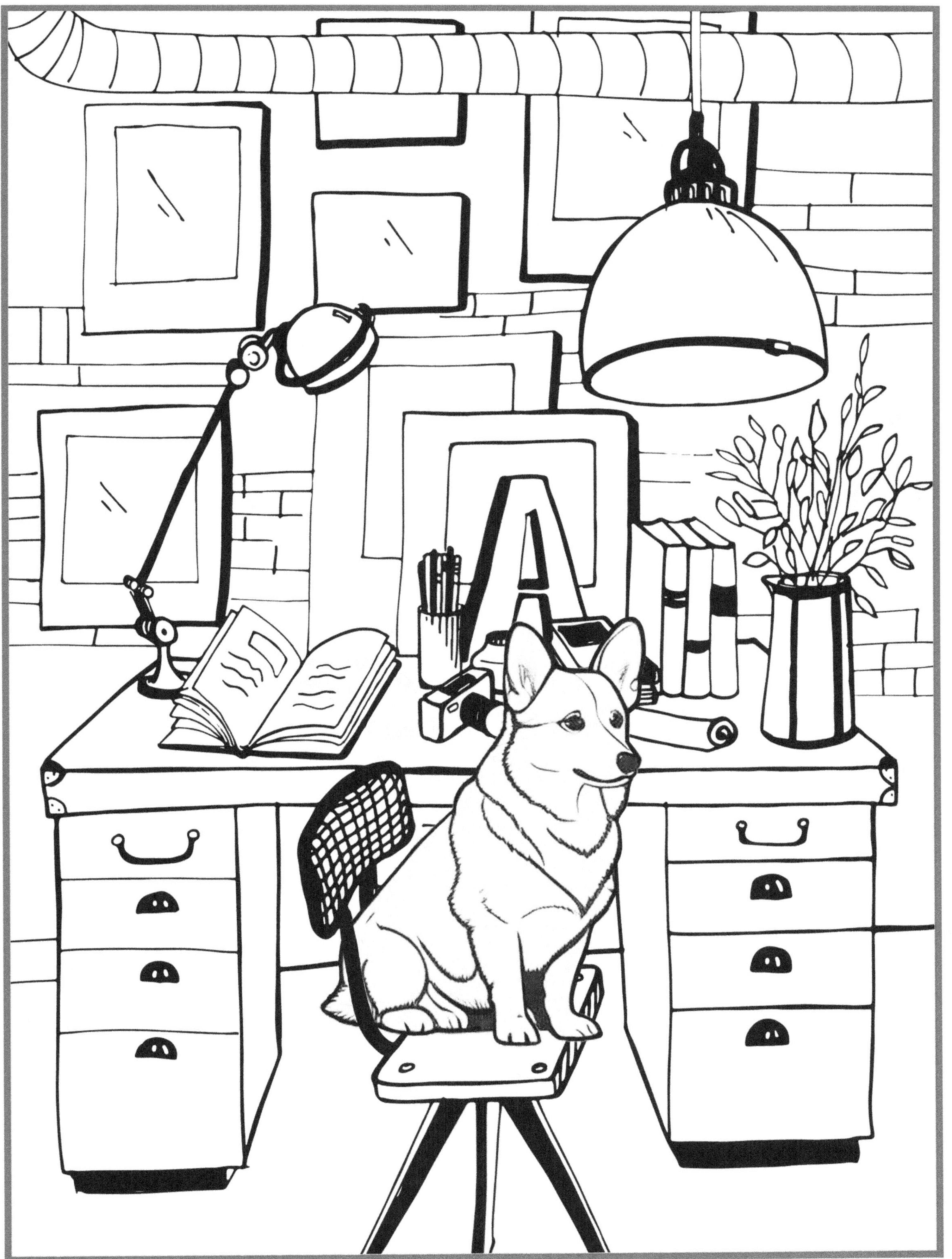

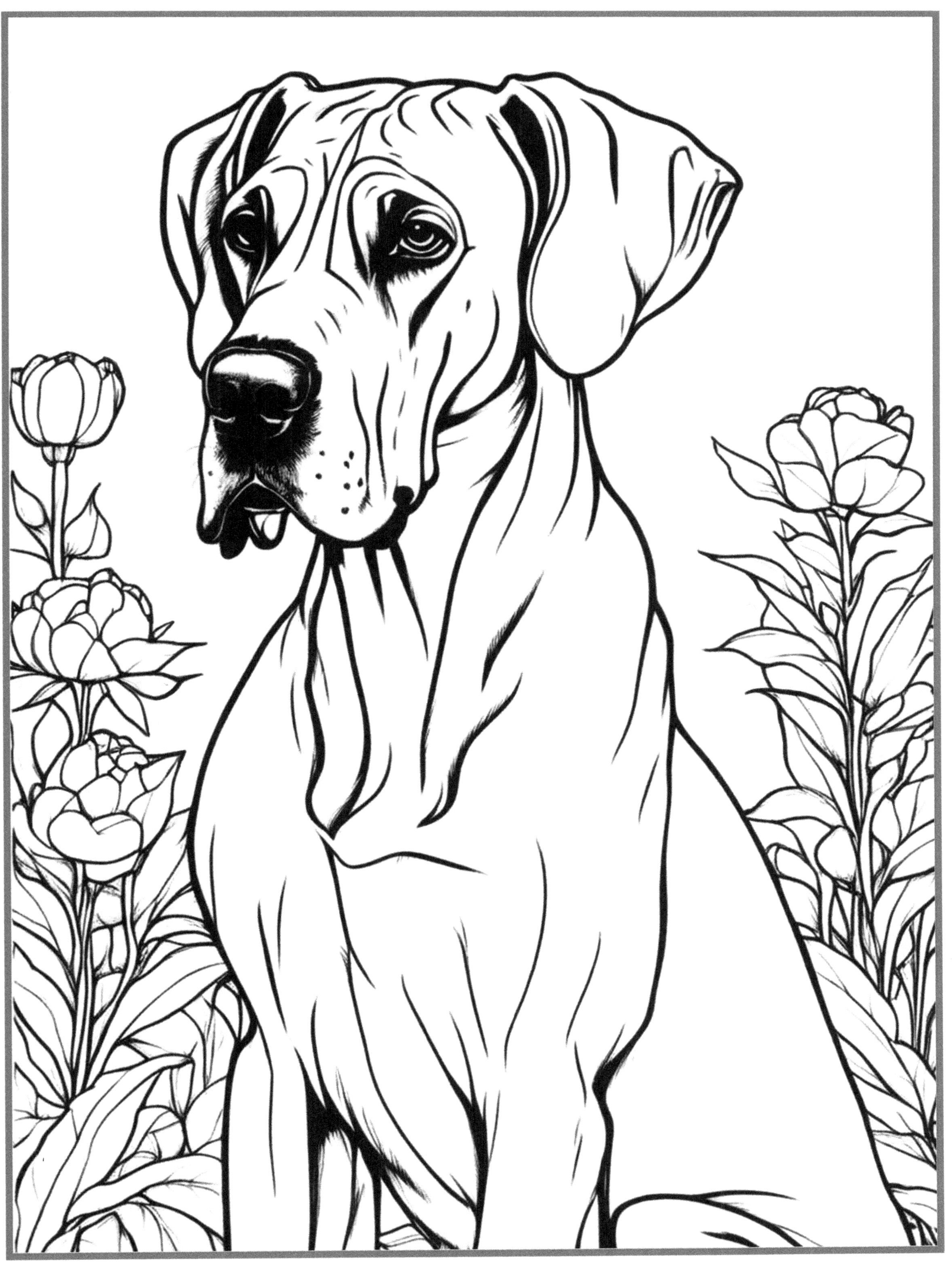

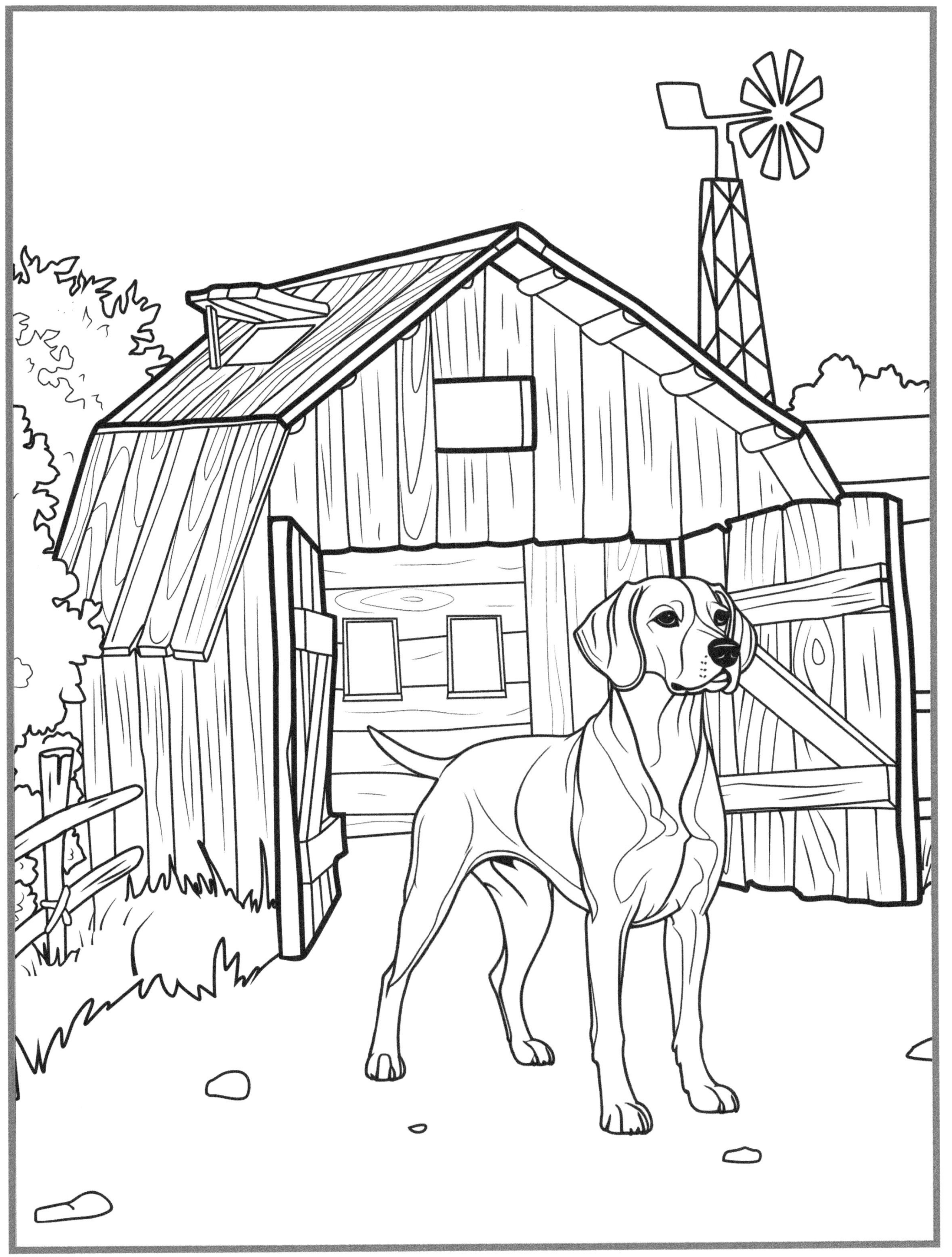

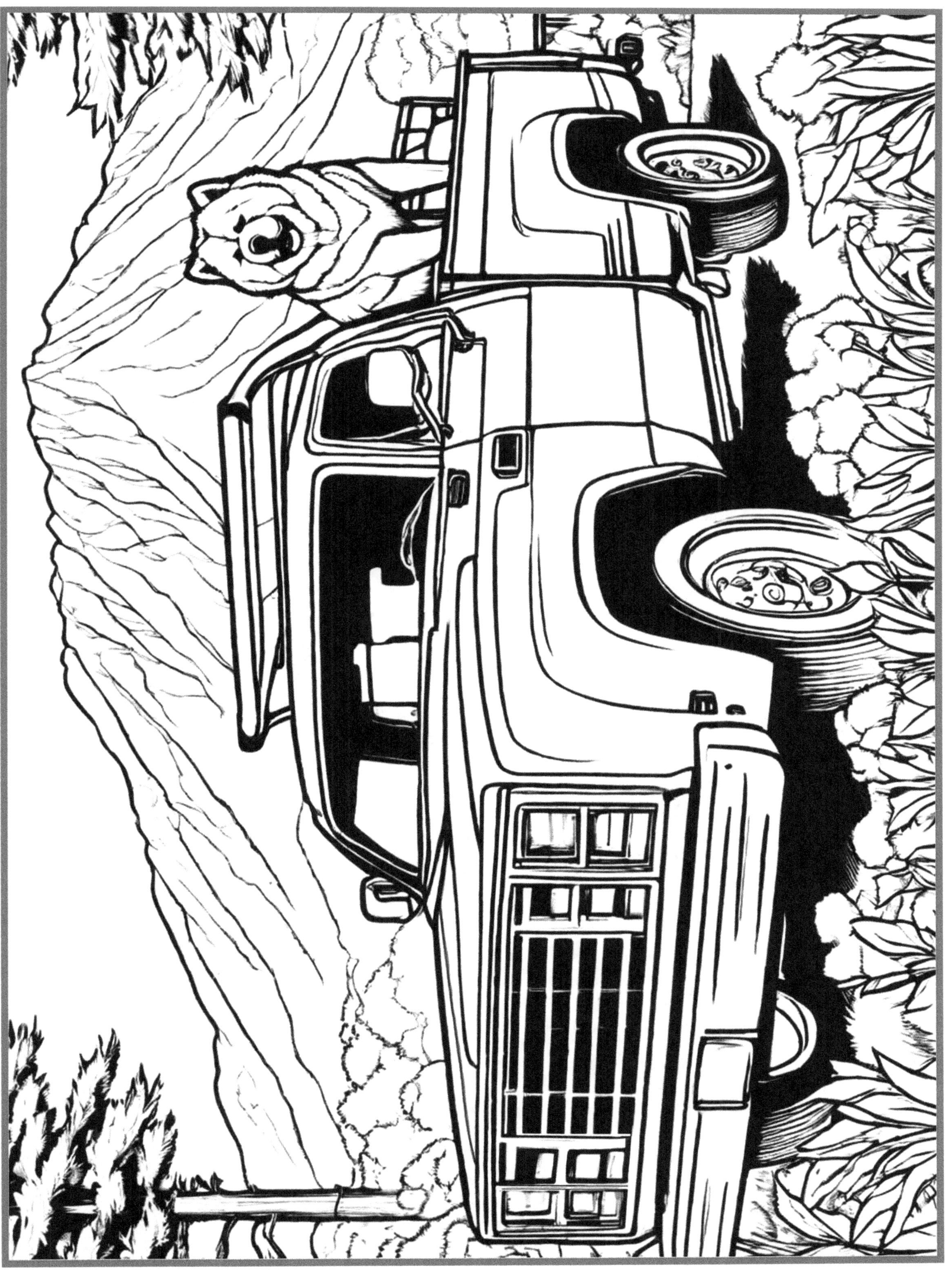

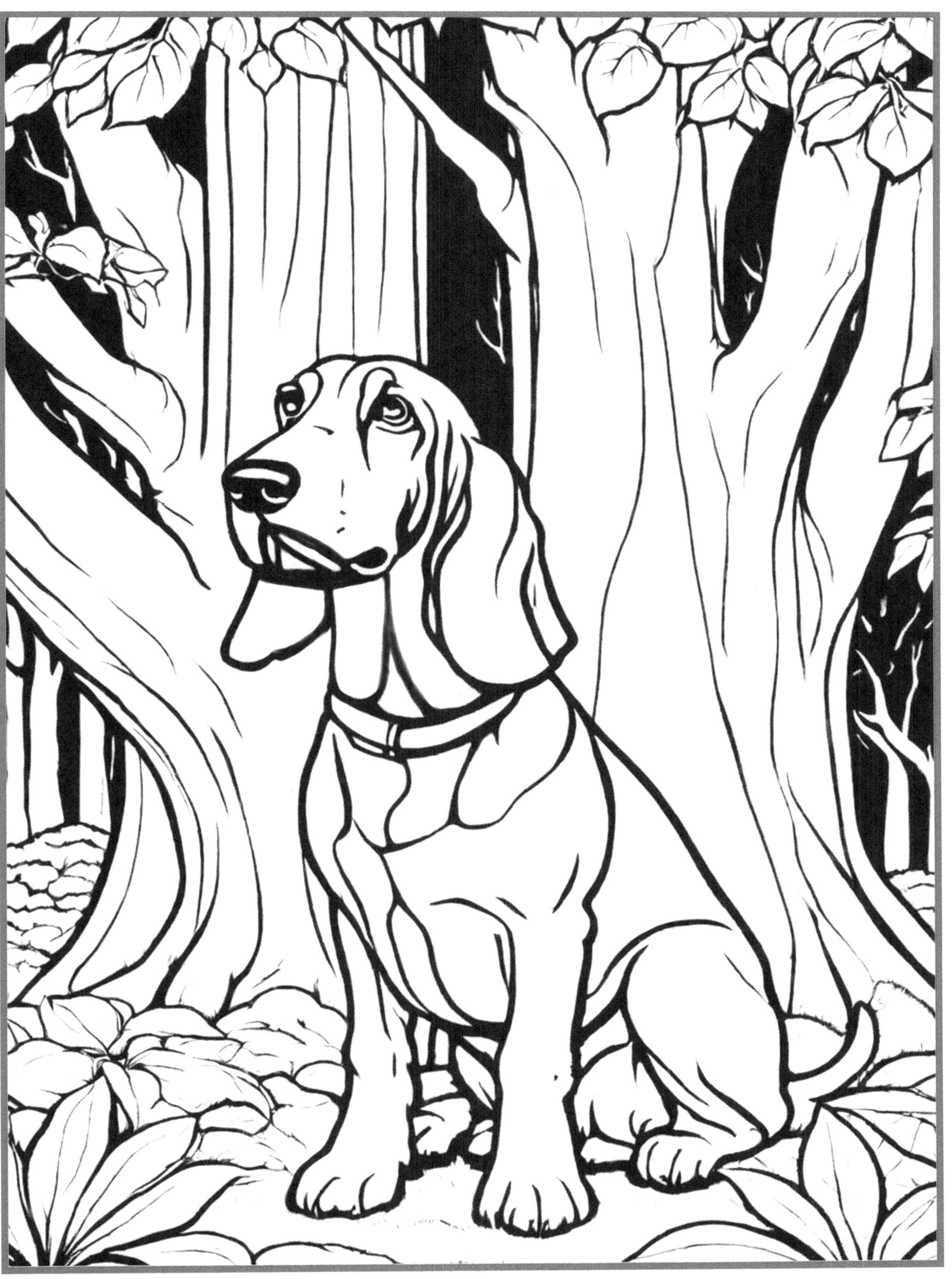

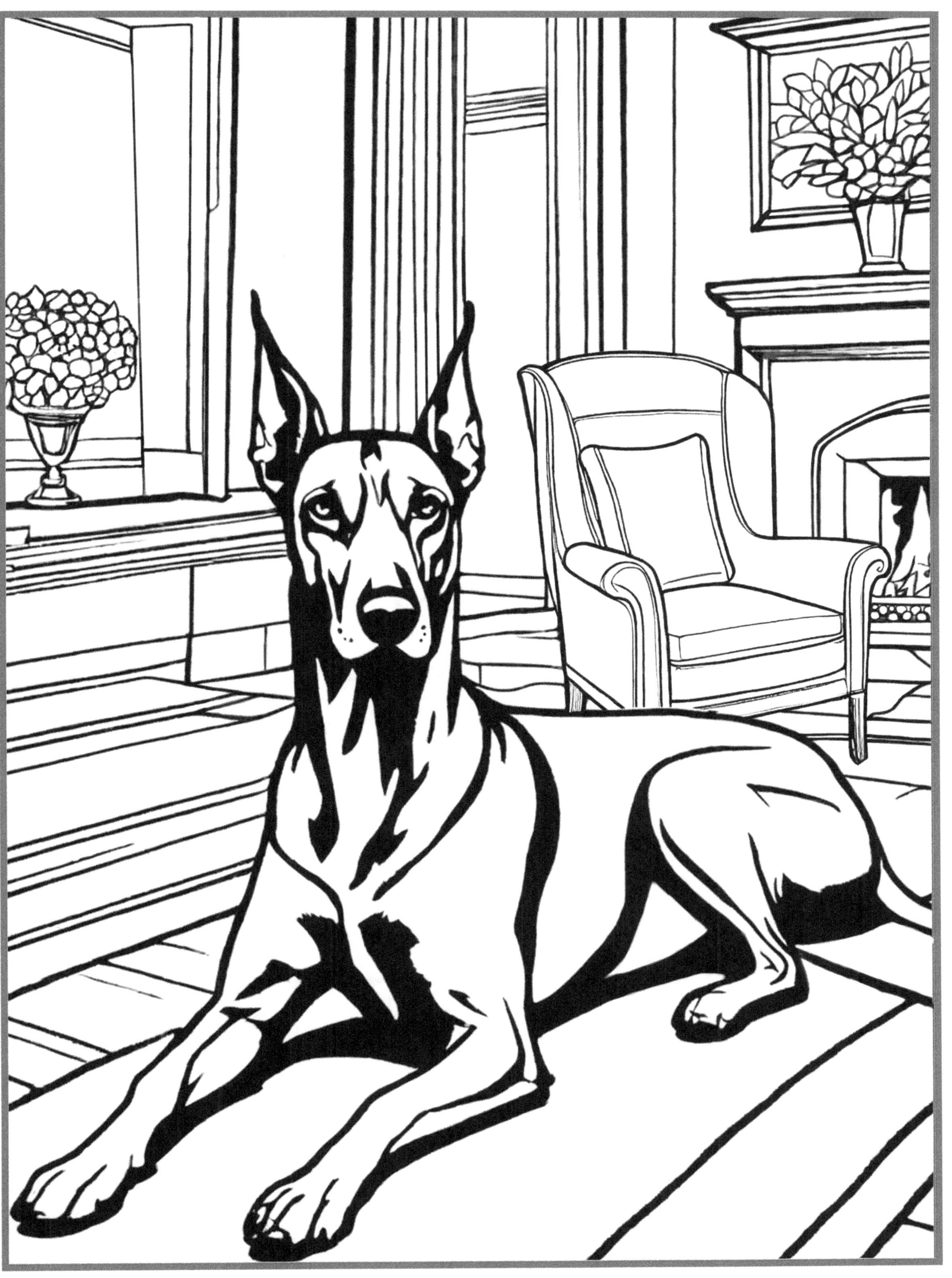

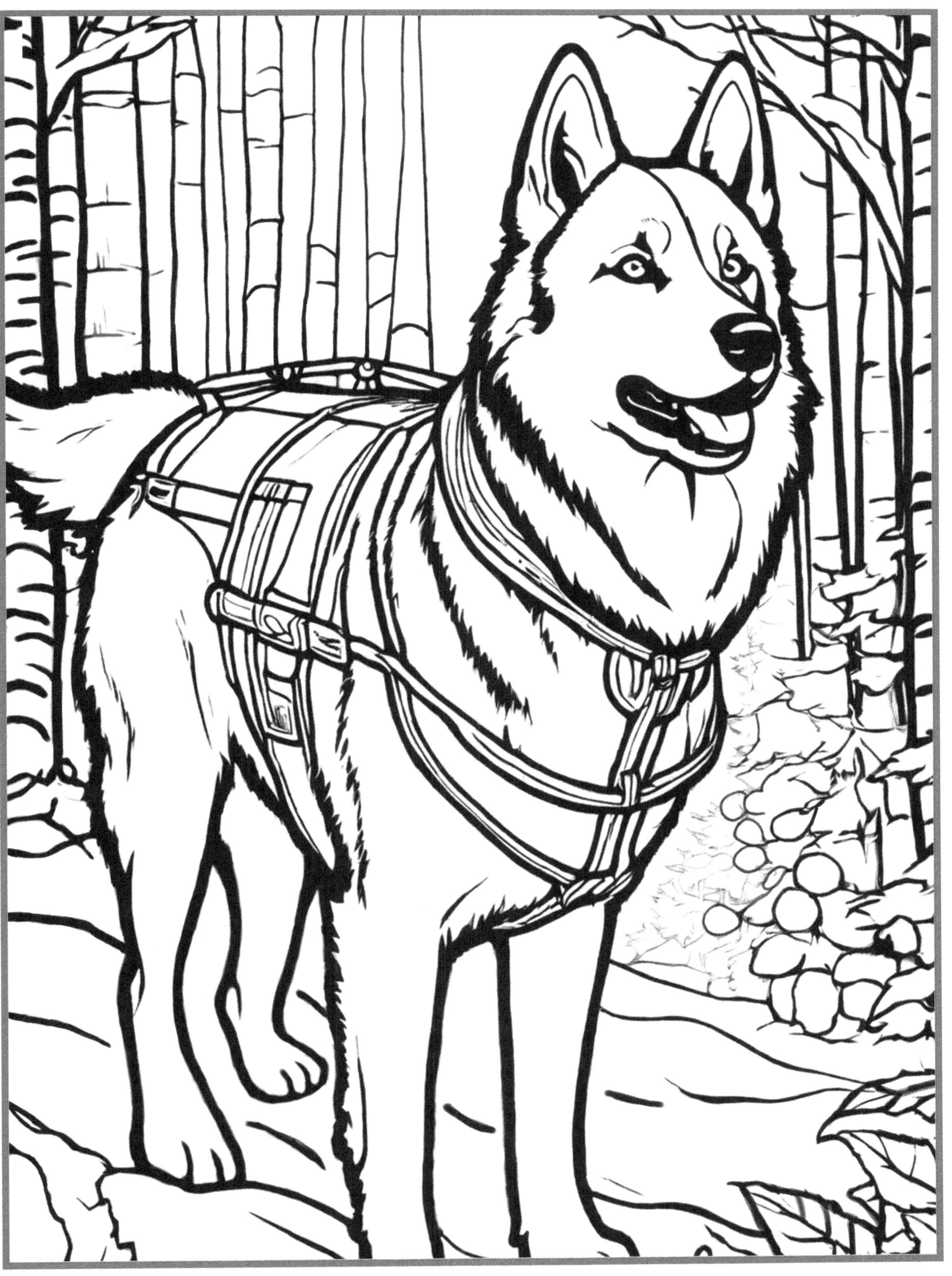

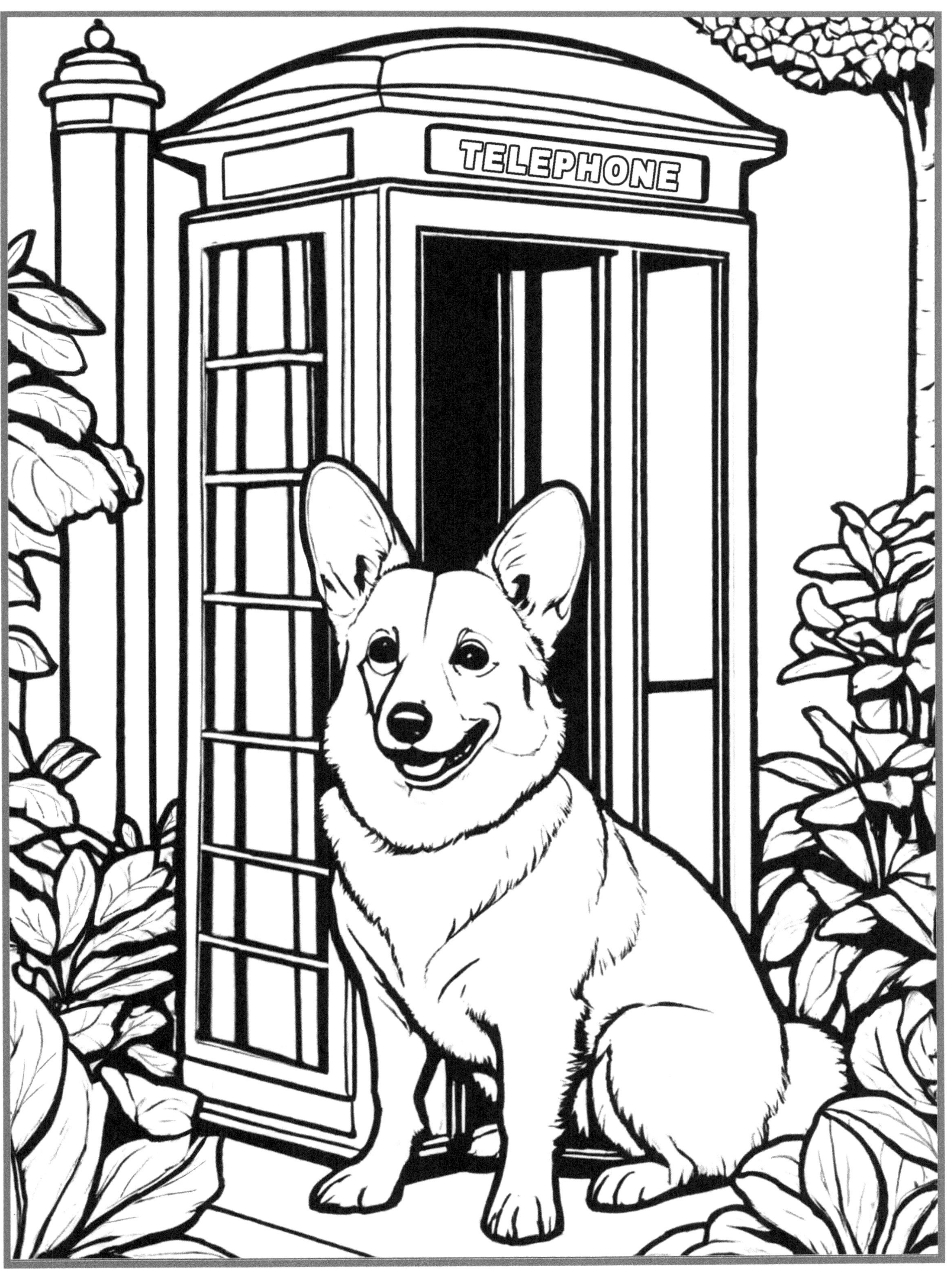
TELEPHONE

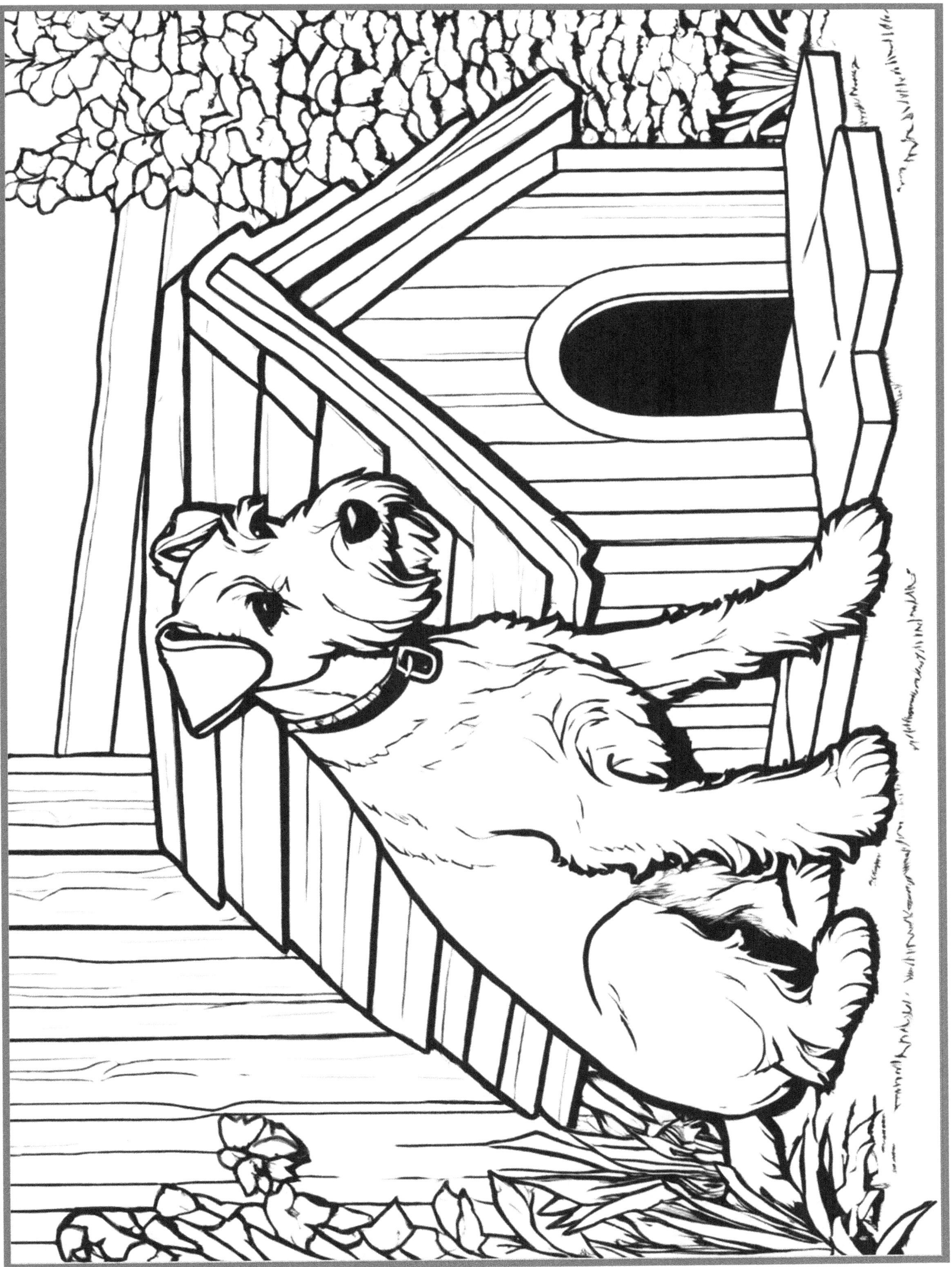

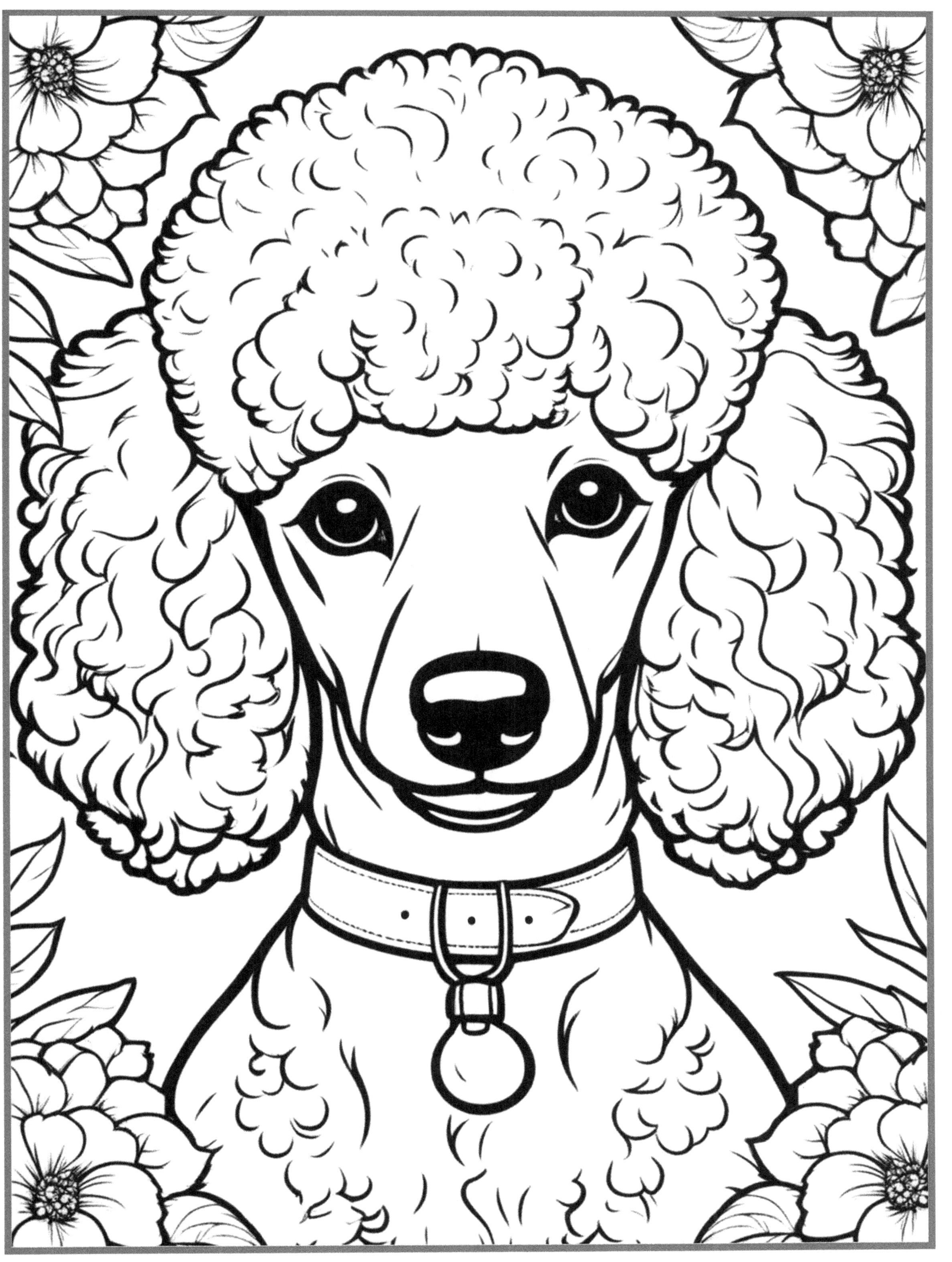

www.ingramcontent.com/pod-product-compliance
Lightning Source LLC
Chambersburg PA
CBHW081225260726
48653CB00010BB/3806

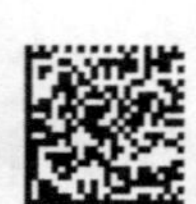
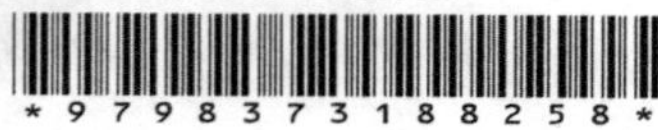